THE STUDY OF TOTAL SOCIETIES

CONTRIBUTORS

Kenneth E. Boulding, Ph.D.
  Professor of Economics, University of Michigan

James S. Coleman, Ph.D.
  Professor of Social Relations, Johns Hopkins University

Amitai Etzioni, Ph.D.
  Associate Professor of Sociology, Columbia University

Abram Kardiner, M.D.
  Former Clinical Professor of Psychiatry, Columbia University

Samuel Z. Klausner, Ed.D., Ph.D.
  Senior Research Associate, Bureau of Social Science Research, Inc.

Marion J. Levy, Jr., Ph.D.
  Professor of Sociology, Princeton University

Ithiel de Sola Pool, Ph.D.
  Professor of Political Science, Massachusetts Institute of Technology

Anatol Rapoport, Ph.D.
  Professor of Mathematical Biology, University of Michigan

Edward A. Tiryakian, Ph.D.
  Associate Professor of Sociology, Duke University

THE STUDY OF
TOTAL SOCIETIES

EDITED, WITH AN INTRODUCTION, BY
SAMUEL Z. KLAUSNER

ANCHOR BOOKS

DOUBLEDAY & COMPANY, INC.

GARDEN CITY, NEW YORK

1967

The Anchor Books edition is the first
publication of *The Study of Total Societies*

Anchor Books edition: 1967

Library of Congress Catalog Card Number 67–12852
Copyright © 1967 by Bureau of Social Science Research
All Rights Reserved
Printed in the United States of America
First Edition

CONTENTS

INTRODUCTION

The nation-state increasingly dominates other forms of human organization. Its boundaries coincide with those of the political and economic institutions that define the national way of life. The culture of these institutions is embodied in political parties, business enterprises, and schools—all of which are now, primarily, subject to the authority of the nation-state. Most significantly, powerful military organizations support the nation-state. Nearly half a century after the establishment of the League of Nations and twenty years after the organization of the United Nations, supranational communities are still groping for an identity.

Social scientists have been intolerant of the vague generalizations, impressionistic reporting, and imprecise evidence associated with the study of large and complex societies. This has tended to discourage the more tough-minded among them from attempting such studies. Twentieth-century anthropologists have preferred to study relatively small settlements, while many sociologists have concentrated on such subgroups as factory workers and street-corner gangs, and many political scientists, on party and governmental organization. Nevertheless, by mid-century, social scientists had been challenged to interpret the grotesque fascist nation-states that proliferated during the 1920s and 1930s, and they are presently challenged to help prevent recurrence of a holocaust such as followed the collisions between the mammoth nation-states during the 1940s.

Some social scientists interpreted these mammoth states as if they were macroscopic extensions of the small groups whose processes and structures they had been studying. There were anthropologists who likened national spending to a giant potlatch, and social psychologists who believed that the righting of distorted perceptions would open the way to international peace. Others, more chastened, interpreted the complex nation-state from the perspective of a particular discipline. Some political scientists looked at the power structure, some sociologists at systems of stratification, while some anthropologists and psychologists co-operated in the study of national character and historians traced either the government or the economy or the culture of a nation through time. In each case, results were bracketed by *ceteris paribus:* these findings hold as long as everything else remains the same. But, as everyone knew, everything else does not remain the same. A change in the class structure implies a change in the flow of investment, which, in turn, implies a change in forms of political influence, which, in turn, may imply a change in the role of the military.

Studies of the nation-state as an integral unit have been appearing. The Yale Political Data Program epitomizes an effort to develop reliable indices or measures of nation-states that would contribute to subsequent theoretical generalizations.[1] Northrop's *The Meeting of East and West*[2] epitomizes a holistic theory of socie-

---

[1] Bruce M. Russett, Hayward R. Alker, Karl W. Deutsch, and Harold D. Lasswell, *World Handbook of Political and Social Indicators* (New Haven: Yale University Press, 1964).

[2] Filmer S. C. Northrop, *The Meeting of East and West* (New York: The Macmillan Co., 1946). This and other macro-sociologies are summarized and criticized in Pitirim A. Sorokin's

ties that might guide subsequent observation and, Northrop hoped, contribute to the reconciliation of those societies.

The present collection of papers is offered to encourage a confluence of these rivulets of total societal studies into the mainstream of American behavioral science. These are contributions toward methodology and theory construction in the study of total societies. The contributors are men who, individually, are officially working in economics, psychiatry, psychology, sociology, and international relations. In practice, each contributor is an interdisciplinarian.

In KENNETH E. BOULDING's writings words such as images, symbols, decision-making, general theory, organization, war and peace, recur. He has given us the term "organizational revolution" to refer to a society's ability to fix its course on the basis of the explicit, quantitative knowledge of social systems now available. Man, Boulding writes, is not limited to simple response to signs, a conditioned behavior. He produces and is a consumer of symbols or images which summarize social values and goals. When ideal and real images diverge to an extent beyond the tolerance of the homeostatic mechanisms, political and personal discontent and, consequently, conflict, become more likely. In *Conflict and Defense*,[3] Boulding discusses the role of mathematical models and game theory in the study of conflict. *Disarmament and the Economy* is a product of his association with the Center for Research in Con-

---

Sociological Theories of Today (New York: Harper and Row, 1966).

[3] Only a selection of each contributor's previous writings will be mentioned in these brief introductions. Full bibliographic references to those publications mentioned are given at the end of this preface.

flict Resolution. His more recent *The Meaning of the Twentieth Century* is a platform for addressing himself to the broader issues of our time. "The Relations of Economic, Political and Social Systems" examines some problems of research on total societies.

JAMES S. COLEMAN, throughout his professional career, has been developing social science methodology. In *Adolescent Society* methods of contextual analysis were used to reveal the influence of social contexts on the behavior and aspirations of high school youth. The program he directs at Johns Hopkins emphasizes mathematical models and computer simulation of social processes. *Models of Change and Response Uncertainty* draws upon his mathematical and survey research interests. He asks whether a given proportion of responses means that that proportion of the population holds this response in a fixed way or that each and every member of the population would respond in that particular way that given proportion of the times. The answer is sought through a tabular analysis of the shifting of responses among respondents over time. *Introduction to Mathematical Sociology* aims to provide "mathematical tools for conceptual elaboration in sociology." Coleman discusses the uses of mathematics in the quantitative description of units, index construction, and for quantitative empirical generalizations about behavior as a language for theory. Disturbed by the habit of assuming that data are normally distributed, he explores the Poisson Distribution as an alternative statistical model for certain kinds of group processes.

Organizational sociology drew the attention of AMITAI ETZIONI early in his professional career (his doctoral dissertation deals with the organizational structure of *kibbutzim*). *A Comparative Analysis of Complex Organizations* offers a cross-institutional basis for comparison of organizations as distinct from the more common cross-cultural perspective. Organizations are classified according to the kind of power they typically employ to control their "lower participants" and the kinds of response this control typically elicits. He conducted a secondary analysis of numerous studies to support his theory that organizations that differ in the kind of power they employ also tend to differ, among other things, in the goals they pursue, their leadership structure, and communication networks. He returned to the same subject in a more popular fashion in his *Modern Organizations*. *Winning Without War*, reflects his association with the Institute of War and Peace Studies at Columbia University. *Political Unification* studies the conditions under which societal units that had previously been autonomous became more intimately related. The theoretical scheme used is a combination of a Parsonian and a cybernetic theory, applied to macroscopic processes. The book is a forerunner of Etzioni's current work on a macro-theory of societal and political processes, of which the paper included here is a preliminary sample.

ABRAM KARDINER has promoted collaboration between psychoanalysis and cultural anthropology for over a quarter of a century. In *The Individual and His Society* he used psychoanalytic concepts to clarify sociological and cultural data. Freud has posited a relatively direct analogy between motivational and social processes. Kardiner recognized how social institutions mediated motivation and behavior. Using Linton's reports on Marquesan and Tanala cultures, Kardiner traced the influence of culture in molding, directing and controlling biological needs. In *The Psychological Frontiers of Society* he applied his method to problems of modern society. "Basic personality"—personality characteristics shared by many members of a given culture due to the imprint of cultural institutions—was introduced as a discipline-bridging concept. In *The Mark of Oppression* he analyzed the character of the American Negro using this concept. Autobiographical and projective data reflected the adaptation of the Negro personality to social oppression. The degree of adaptation was expressed not as an individual psychological but as a sociological variable, the "incidence pattern of intropsychic accommodation."

SAMUEL Z. KLAUSNER's interests in personality research, the sociological study of roles, and the study of religious institutions were combined in his work on the religio-psychiatric movement reported in *Psychiatry and Religion*. The work describes the adaptation of pastors to scientifically conceived psychotherapy and of psychiatrists to religious conceptions of healing. *The Quest for Self-Control* reviewed psychological, sociological and cultural theories, and research on human behavior in stressful situations. A recent article, "Some Notes on the Production of Psychiatric and Psychological Knowledge," an empirical study in the sociology of knowledge, examines the impact of work context and personality on the research methods of behavioral scientists.

MARION J. LEVY, JR. explored the relation of the family to other social institutions in *The Family Revolution in Modern China*. Structural-functional analysis was used to evaluate the impact of industrialization on the family in "traditional" and "transitional" China. Levy delineates five structural requisites of a kinship system:

role differentiation; solidarity; economic allocation, integration and expression; and political allocation *in* the kinship structure. In *The Structure of Society* he introduced "a general conceptual scheme for beginning the comparative analysis of societies." The structural requisites of a kinship system were here delineated for a total society. Methodological problems of this type of analysis were set forth in "The Logical Nature of An Action Scheme." The theoretical analysis of total societies continues in his recently published *Modernization and the Structure of Societies.*

ITHIEL DE SOLA POOL's substantive interest in the symbols of political propaganda led to his concern with methodological tools for exploring the nature of propaganda. Earlier, his work applied content analysis, and later he became involved in problems of computer simulation. *The Prestige Papers*, a product of the Hoover Institute, reports a content analysis of political symbols in some leading newspapers of Great Britain, Russia, France, Germany, and the United States at various periods. *Trends in Content Analysis,* a work he edited, reflected a more sophisticated approach to content analysis than generally current in the field. Here, the quantitative method was applied to exploration of emotional states, linguistics, and history. His recent *Candidates, Issues and Strategies* tells how he and his colleagues of Simulatics Corporation developed computer simulation techniques for extrapolating election information while studying the 1960 presidential election.

ANATOL RAPOPORT has been applying mathematical thinking to biological, psychological and sociological problems. During the late forties he contributed to the mathematical theory of neural nets and of motivation.

At that time he thought of himself as a logical positivist. Writing on semantics, he called attention to the fallacy of separating science and values. In *Science and the Goals of Man* one discerns his interest in conflict and decision processes. Rapoport proposed that conflict be undercut by general assent to a value system which would give human agreement priority over human disagreement. The publication of *Operational Philosophy* in 1953 marked a modification in his positivistic thinking which he describes as leaving the "austere conservatism of logical positivism." Instead, the constructive aspects of symbolism as represented in the writings of Whitehead, Cassirer, Langer, and Burke were given greater prominence. Like Dewey, Rapoport was concerned with the relation between thinking and doing. *Fights, Games and Debates* contributed to the mathematization of social science in general and to game theory in particular. His more recent *Strategy and Conscience* reviews theories of rational decision-making under conditions of uncertainty and criticizes the tendency of military planners to rely on probability statements in formulating national strategy.

EDWARD A. TIRYAKIAN has been a philosophically and, especially, an ethically concerned sociologist. *Sociologism and Existentialism: Two Perspectives on the Individual and Society,* dedicated to Jacques Maritain and Pitirim Sorokin, reviewed the points of contact between sociology and philosophy in epistemology, and in the sociologies of knowledge, science and art. Some existentialist views of society as hostile to the authentic nature of the individual constitute obstacles to rapprochement, but the convergence of society and existential philosophy is illustrated in Jaspers' and

Durkheim's common concern with transcendence, with being-in-society as an intrinsic existential structure of human being. The complementarity of existential phenomenology and sociology was spelled out in "Existential Phenomenology and the Sociological Tradition." Recently Tiryakian edited a *festschrift* for Sorokin entitled *Sociological Theory, Values and Sociocultural Change.* Tiryakian's theoretical concern has been with the structuration and destructuration of total societies as phenomena of social existence.

Thus, each contributor has been an articulator of diverse disciplines: Boulding spans economics, mathematics and sociology; Coleman relates mathematics and sociology; Etzioni, organizational sociology and international relations; Kardiner, psychiatry and anthropology; Klausner, sociology and psychology; Levy, social theory and Sinology; Pool, sociology and political science; Rapoport, biology, mathematics, philosophy, psychology, and sociology; and Tiryakian, sociology and philosophy. They were chosen as men familiar with the problems of bridging disciplines to build an image of a total society. Earlier versions of their papers were presented at a conference held in Washington, D.C., on July 28 and 29, 1965, under the auspices of the Bureau of Social Science Research, Inc. That conference and this report were sponsored by the Army Research Office of the Department of the Army through the Special Operations Research Office of American University, as a part of SORO's long-term research interests in the problems of analyzing societies.

The editor appreciates the help of many persons at various stages of conference organization and report preparation. Dr. Theodore Vallance, Director of

SORO, and the late Dr. Rex D. Hopper and Mr. Edward W. Gude, also of SORO, originally conceived the conference and monitored the contract for SORO. Dr. Jessie Bernard was a frequent consultant. Brigadier General Frederick P. Munson (USA, ret.) of SORO and Mr. John R. Taylor, Executive Officer of the Bureau of Social Science Research, Inc., helped to solve many administrative problems.

Précis of the discussions were prepared by Dr. Elisabeth Crawford, Dr. Louise Johnson, Mrs. Ann Richardson, and Mr. George Zollschan, all research associates of the Bureau of Social Science Research. Especial appreciation is expressed to Dr. Robert T. Bower, Director of the Bureau of Social Science Research, who created and maintains the organizational structure and the atmosphere of free inquiry in which such a conference is possible. The reader of this volume will be indebted to Anne Freedgood of Doubleday and Company, who added polish to the English style of the original manuscripts. And, a husband's praises to Madeleine Zipporah, who "looks well to the ways of her household and does not eat the bread of idleness."

Samuel Z. Klausner

Washington, D.C.
August 30, 1966

SELECTED WORKS OF THE CONTRIBUTORS

Boulding, Kenneth E. *Conflict and Defense.* New York: Harper & Bros., 1962.

——. "The Relations of Economic, Political and Social Systems," *Social and Economic Studies,* Vol. 11, No. 4 (December 1962), pp. 351–62.

——, and Benoit, Emile (eds.). *Disarmament and the Economy.* New York: Harper & Row, 1963.

——. *The Meaning of the Twentieth Century.* New York: Harper & Row, 1964.

Coleman, James S. *Adolescent Society.* Glencoe, Ill.: The Free Press of Glencoe, 1961.

——. *Introduction to Mathematical Sociology.* New York: The Free Press of Glencoe, 1964.

——. *Models of Change and Response Uncertainty.* Englewood Cliffs, N.J.: Prentice-Hall, 1965.

Etzioni, Amitai. *A Comparative Analysis of Complex Organizations.* Glencoe, Ill.: The Free Press of Glencoe, 1961.

——. *Modern Organizations.* Englewood Cliffs, N.J.: Prentice-Hall, 1964.

——. *Winning Without War.* Garden City, N.Y.: Doubleday & Company, 1964.

——. *Political Unification.* New York: Holt, Rinehart and Winston, 1965.

Kardiner, Abram. *The Individual and His Society.* New York: Columbia University Press, 1939.

—— (with others). *The Psychological Frontiers of Society.* New York: Columbia University Press, 1945.

——, and Ovesey, L. *The Mark of Oppression: Explorations in the Personality of the American Negro.* Cleveland: World Publishing Co. (Meridian Press), 1961. Originally published 1951.

Klausner, Samuel Z. *Psychiatry and Religion.* New York: The Free Press of Glencoe, 1964.

———— (ed.). *The Quest for Self-Control.* New York: The Free Press, 1965.

————. "Some Notes on the Production of Psychiatric and Psychological Knowledge," *Journal of Consulting Psychology,* Vol. 29, No. 5 (October 1965), pp. 404–14.

Levy, Marion J., Jr. *The Family Revolution in Modern China.* Cambridge, Mass.: Harvard University Press, 1949.

————. *The Structure of Society.* Princeton: Princeton University Press, 1952.

————, (with Kochen, M.). "The Logical Nature of an Action Scheme," *Behavioral Science,* Vol. 1, No. 4 (October 1956), pp. 265–89.

————. *Modernization and the Structure of Societies.* Princeton: Princeton University Press, 1966.

Pool, Ithiel de Sola. *The Prestige Papers: A Survey of Their Editorials.* Stanford, Calif.: Stanford University (Hoover Institute), 1952.

———— (ed.). *Trends in Content Analysis.* Urbana, Ill.: University of Illinois Press, 1959.

————, and others. *Candidates, Issues and Strategies: A Computer Simulation of the 1960 and 1964 Elections.* Cambridge, Mass.: Massachusetts Institute of Technology Press, 1965.

Rapoport, Anatol. *Science and the Goals of Man.* New York: Harper & Bros., 1950.

————. *Operational Philosophy.* New York: Harper & Bros., 1953.

————. *Fights, Games and Debates.* Ann Arbor: The University of Michigan Press, 1960.

————. *Strategy and Conscience.* New York: Harper & Row, 1964.

Tiryakian, Edward A. *Sociologism and Existentialism: Two*

Perspectives on the Individual and Society. Englewood Cliffs, N.J.: Prentice-Hall, Inc., 1962.

————. *Sociological Theory, Values and Sociocultural Change: Essays in Honor of Pitirim A. Sorokin*. New York: The Free Press of Glencoe, 1963.

————. "Existential Phenomenology and the Sociological Tradition," *American Sociological Review*, Vol. 30, No. 5 (October 1965), pp. 674–88.

METHODOLOGY

SAMUEL Z. KLAUSNER

LINKS AND MISSING LINKS
BETWEEN THE SCIENCES OF MAN

INTERDISCIPLINARY STATEMENTS IN THE STUDY OF TOTAL
SOCIETIES

THE TOTAL STUDY OF TOTAL SOCIETIES?

The term "total society" may be used to refer to an
ecologically delimited, more or less interdependent set
of human collectivities. The student of a total society
could inquire into the spatial and/or organizational interdependence of events. He could report the impact
of a society's northern upon its southern region, of its
army upon its factories, and of its ethnic groups upon
its political parties. The term "total" indicates an intent to consider all of the people in that particular
area. In practice, the student of a total society studies
enough of the area and enough of the people so that
his judgments about the entirety suffer no more than
some tolerable error.

A "total study" of a society would cut across these
concrete spatial and organizational segments with conceptions abstracted according to the rules of disciplines
such as psychology, sociology, anthropology, and geog-
raphy.[1] A re-articulation of these disciplinary abstractions is a *sine qua non* for describing a total society at
a point in time, predicting its state at some later time,

[1] Talcott Parsons, *The Structure of Social Action* (Glencoe,
Ill.: The Free Press, 1947).

and specifying the mechanisms involved in the change of state.[2] Theoretically, a "total study" is not realizable in practice because of the unlimited number of possible disciplinary perspectives. In practice, a student concerned with a total study selects that minimum of relevant variables from a minimum number of disciplines which enable him to predict phenomena with no more than some tolerable error. In bringing together the contributions of various disciplines, he states relationships between events conceptualized from several perspectives. This paper is concerned with some problems arising in an attempt to forge a "total study of a total society" by articulating concepts abstracted from differing disciplinary perspectives.

This paper begins by noting and then rejecting the argument that there are no real distinctions between behavioral science disciplines and that, therefore, there is no real problem in articulating events from these several perspectives. Several recent attempts at integrating the contributions of the various disciplines—of psychology and sociology, or of economics and political science—are then mentioned. Parsons' action theory is proposed as a frame of reference useful for examining propositions which combine variables from disparate disciplines. The second part of the paper sets forth general conditions for a "good" bi-disciplinary proposition. Then, with the aid of illustrations from interdisciplinary studies, it is argued that a "good" bi-disciplinary statement must indicate some mechanism which shows how action relevant at one conceptual level affects events conceptualized on another level.

[2] Ernst Cassirer, *The Philosophy of Symbolic Forms*, Vol. III: *The Phenomenology of Knowledge* (New Haven: Yale University Press, 1957).

EPIPHENOMENALISM OR SEPARATE DISCIPLINES

Ancient statements relating planetary movements and human motives, and some more recent ones relating climate and character, make some scientists skeptical about relating occurrences in two different domains. Two arguments are advanced in defense of such skepticism. First, an apparent relationship—say, between stars and motives—is either an exercise in fantasy or an inference from an improbable coincidence. The scientist insisting on "meaningful" correlations and inferences based on an adequate sample of occurrences is not deterred by this argument. Second, if events in one domain are shown to be functions of events in a second domain—say, motives are a function of placement in the social structure—then are the concepts of at least one of those not superfluous for the understanding of human behavior? This charge of "reductionism" or "epiphenomenalism" is rejected by Emile Durkheim. Durkheim takes his illustration from propositions purporting to relate psychological and physiological concepts. He contends that were one to accept the contention that "the memory is solely a property of the tissues, there is no mental life [and] no real field for psychology." Mental phenomena, being epiphenomenal to the physical world, would simply replicate physical laws. Durkheim suggests that mental processes are produced through the interactions of mental elements. This produces a domain of mental phenomena *sui generis,* with laws of their own. Similarly, he argues for a *sui generis* social reality which is analytically independent of a psychological substrate.[3]

[3] "Individual and Collective Representations" in Durkheim's *Sociology and Philosophy,* trans. D. F. Pocock (Glencoe, Ill.:

On the other hand, it would be inconceivable that psychological and sociological variables would be independent of one another since both are aspects of the same concrete behavioral events. A model of a "total society," while recognizing the distinctness of various theoretical levels, must be concerned with statements which link a term on one level with a term on another. Economic factors must be related to personality factors and a change in religious institutions related to a change in political institutions. The issue becomes one of identifying transformation concepts which link concepts on two or more theoretical levels. These transformation concepts will refer to "mechanisms" by which a change in the economy affects personality or a change in religion affects the secular polity.

ATTEMPTS TO INTEGRATE DISCIPLINES

Various methods have been used to arrive at valid interdisciplinary statements. One approach has been to focus upon a sufficiently abstract level so that principles of structure and change among events become formal principles which hold irrespective of the substantive content which is so ordered. Perhaps Alfred North Whitehead has presented the most comprehensive effort in this direction. He develops a general notion of organism such that "everything of which we are conscious, as enjoyed, perceived, willed, or thought, shall have the character of a particular instance of the general scheme."[4] An organism may be a society of indi-

---

The Free Press, 1953). Durkheim takes some pains in *Le Suicide* (Paris: Felix Alcan, 1897) to demonstrate that the "suicide rate," a societal attribute, cannot be predicted from psychological attributes such as individual depressive states.

[4] *Process and Reality* (New York: The Macmillan Co., 1929), p. 4.

viduals or a society of body cells. Nexus is a general concept of connections between events at any level.

A more substantively oriented attempt is developed by the authors of *The International Encyclopedia of Unified Science*.[5] Charles Morris, for example, in his contribution to the encyclopedia entitled "Theory of Signs," treats science as a form of discourse. The body of knowledge called science consists of a set of statements formulated according to the rules of a relatively generic language. Each special science constitutes a specific language. Any language may be thought of as consisting of signs, objects, and behavioral events. The behavioral events are responses to signs and define the meaning of the objects which the signs represent. The study of the relations among signs, objects, and behaviors he calls semiotics. Semiotics is offered as a metatheory of the interrelations among scientific concepts.[6] Interdisciplinary integration through a unifying language is pushed to the extreme by Alfred Korzybski.[7] Semantics, or more specifically, the study of symbolic relations, bridges the natural and the cultural sciences as well as providing a unifying model for the cultural sciences.

A third approach assembles statements of each special discipline about the society, as one would assemble bricks and mortar in building a house. A study of a "total society" from this point of view consists of parallel but separate individual disciplinary studies of the

[5] Otto Neurath, *et al.* (eds.), Vol. I (Chicago: University of Chicago Press, 1955).

[6] Semiotics has three divisions: the relation of signs and objects defines the field of semantics; the relation of signs and behavioral interpretations defines pragmatics; and the relation among the signs constitutes syntactics.

[7] *Science and Sanity* (Lakeville, Conn.: The International Non-Aristotelian Library Publishing Co., 1933).

8 *Methodology*

society. For example, a series of books on nation-states, based heavily on data from the Human Relations Area Files, records relevant statements on the economy, religion, family life, agriculture, and so forth, of each society. These volumes do not present "total study" models of societies in an organic fashion since each discipline is treated separately. For example, economic factors are not especially related to religious, familial, or agricultural factors. George Murdock[8] has taken the additional step of establishing such interdisciplinary propositions using data from the Human Relations Area Files. He correlates, for example, family and economic patterns through ratings on both dimensions for a series of societies. These propositions do not present an integrated interdisciplinary model of a single total society. Rather, they are nomothetic statements which express the general correlation of, say, familial and economic factors in a number of societies.

Attempts to understand a total society by co-ordinating the contributions of a series of disciplines have been dwarfed by the emergence of new interdisciplinary, usually bi-disciplinary, sciences. Physical chemistry, biochemistry, and biophysics in the natural sciences are paralleled by social psychology, political economy, and culture *and* personality in the behavioral sciences. These areas are not yet, strictly speaking, disciplines. There is no physical-chemical theory, but there is physical theory and chemical theory, and certain problem areas such as that of radio isotopes which draw upon both. A social psychology text tends to consist of a series of topics elucidated by both sociological and psychological concepts rather than a set of propositions cumulated into a theoretical network.

[8] *Social Structure* (New York: The Macmillan Co., 1949).

Some topics are, however, emerging as interdisciplinary theory fragments. Socialization, for example, maps the relation between the structure of society and the structure of personalities that develop in that society.

PARSONS' GENERAL THEORY OF ACTION AS AN INTERDISCIPLINARY APPROACH

Talcott Parsons, in a series of works on the theory of action, exemplifies a fourth approach to the articulation of disciplines.[9] Parsons' theory of action is substantive. Its terms refer not to the language or symbols of science but to aspects of the behavioral events themselves. It is not at so high a level of abstraction as to be a formal theory of all relations but is at a sufficiently high level of abstraction to span the psychological, social, and cultural sciences. Concrete acts of human beings provide the starting point for all the social sciences. Each discipline is a peculiar perspective on these acts, an abstraction from them with reference to its own orientation. Action itself becomes a perspectival or abstract concept and a system of action is the set of abstractions from some particular perspective. The interconnections of the actions of an individual constitute the personality system. The social system abstracts from the process of interaction between two or more actors; the interaction process as such is the focus of the social perspective. A cultural system is constituted by the organization of the values, norms, and symbols which guide the choices made by the actors.

[9] *The Social System* (Glencoe, Ill.: The Free Press, 1951); and Talcott Parsons and Edward A. Shils (eds.), *Toward a General Theory of Action* (Cambridge, Mass.: Harvard University Press, 1951), p. 54 f.

Traditional distinctions among disciplinary specialists correspond roughly with one or another of these systems. Psychologists study personality; sociologists, the social system; and anthropologists, the cultural system.

A "total study" of a "total society" focuses primarily on the social system and its subsystems. According to Parsons and Smelser, "a society is the theoretically limiting case of the social system which, in its subsystems, comprises *all* of the important roles of the persons and collectivities composing its population."[10] Personality and cultural systems are of concern insofar as they are linked with social systems. The subsystems of the social system are differentiated according to their contributions to the working of the broader system. Parsons distinguishes four such functions. The adaptive subsystem involves processes which deal with the broader system's subjection to stressful inputs. Included in the adaptive subsystem are orientations toward this environment, and the means for coping with the environment which enable the system to attain its goals. In the case of a society, the *economy* makes these types of contributions to the solution of adaptive problems.

A second subsystem consists of those activities which contribute to the broader system's goal attainment. This system is organized around the mobilization of the prerequisites for the attainment of system goals, especially the organization of power. The organization of power orders the relation between a system and its environment. In the case of a society, the *polity* functions in this way.

The *integrative* subsystem involves the patterning of

[10] Talcott Parsons and Neil J. Smelser, *Economy and Society: A Study of the Integration of Economic and Social Theory* (New York: The Free Press of Glencoe, 1964 [originally published 1956]).

relationships among actors within the broader system and the articulation of cultural value patterns with motivations of individual actors. In the case of a society, integrative functions are performed by certain aspects of religious institutions, stratification systems, and mechanisms of social control.

The adaptive, goal attainment and integrative subsystems involve processes of interaction among members of the society, or between them and members of other societies. A fourth system serves as a dual resource for all three of those interactive systems. One of its functions is *pattern maintenance*, the maintaining of general cultural patterns from which the other systems draw specific norms and values. In the case of a society, pattern maintenance functions are subserved by the family, educational institutions, and the value-conserving aspects of religious tradition. A second function of this system is the maintenance of motivation to act of actors in the interactive systems. This includes management of stresses which might affect the allocation of individual and social energies. Its second function is *tension management*. In the case of a society, tension management functions are also subserved by family, educational, and religious institutions, and especially through the healing functions of these and the specific healing institutions.

These social subsystems correspond roughly to academic specialties, though not clearly to contemporary departmental lines. Political scientists concentrate on government and international relations and the problems of power which constitute the polity. Economists deal with problems of investment, entrepreneurship, producing and marketing organizations which constitute the economy. There are special students of the family and of educational and psychotherapeutic insti-

tutions which are involved in pattern maintenance and
tension management functions, and special students of
religion, social stratification, and social control—the institutions and mechanisms involved in integrative functions.

CONDITIONS FOR A "GOOD" BI-DISCIPLINARY STATEMENT

Most research of psychologists and sociologists or of
specialists in the family or in religious institutions re-
volves about intrasystemic or, using the academic distinctions, intradisciplinary statements. A "total society"
may also include many intradisciplinary statements.
However, it must go beyond this to statements relating
concepts of many disciplines. The simplest case is that
of a statement which relates concepts from but two disciplines at a time. This paper will deal only with this
simplest case of bi-disciplinary propositions.

A good bi-disciplinary statement satisfies two conditions. The first of these guarantees that it is bi-disciplinary. Each of its two principal variables belongs to a
different system or subsystem: one referring to personality and the other to the social system; or one referring
to the economy and the other to the polity. The second
condition is that the variables in the two systems be
mediated by a third variable, the role of which is to
transform a concept at one system level or referring to
one type of system function to a concept at another
system level or referring to another type of system
function. Lacking this mediating or transforming variable or concept, the relation between the two systems
would either be "unexplained," a mere co-occurrence,
or the systems would be isomorphic. In the latter case,

the requirement that the concepts have distinct system references would not be met.

A bi-disciplinary statement must take account of the fact that each of its main variables is defined by its position in a network of variables on its own system level. This is what is meant by a consistent and closed theoretical system. The principal function of the transforming concept is to refer to a process which takes into consideration the different principles of conceptual organization on the two levels or the different functional orientations of the two subsystems. In the following discussion, expressions such as "the link between culture and personality" will be used elliptically to refer to a link between a concept which refers to the norms or values inherent in some concrete act, and a concept which refers to the relation of that particular act to a particular individual's needs, feelings, cognitions, or predispositions to behave.

EXAMPLES OF BI-DISCIPLINARY STATEMENTS

SOURCES OF EXAMPLES

A number of examples of bi-disciplinary propositions were collected. Most were from books widely read by social scientists. Erik H. Erikson's *Young Man Luther*[11] was used as a source of propositions linking personality and culture. David C. McClelland's *The Achieving Society*[12] provided examples of propositions linking personality and the economy. Joseph Schumpeter's *Capitalism, Socialism and Democracy*[13] and John C.

[11] New York: W. W. Norton Co., 1958.
[12] New York: D. Van Nostrand Co., 1961.
[13] New York: Harper and Bros., 1962.

Campbell's *Defense of the Middle East*[14] supplied propositions linking the economy and the polity. Salo W. Baron's *Modern Nationalism and Religion*[15] supplied propositions relating the polity and religious institutions. A potpourri of propositions was garnered from Arnold Toynbee's *A Study of History* (Somervell abridgment)[16] and from Ibn Khaldun's classic *Muquaddimah.*[17]

LINKING PERSONALITY AND SOCIETY

A personality and social variable may be joined in a bi-disciplinary statement. One way of mediating the two system levels, accounting for their linkage, is to cite a concrete organizational structure in which the transformation takes place. Following are some examples of statements linking personality and the social system.

McClelland states that n-achievement, a personality variable characteristic of individuals, is positively correlated with an economic subsystem variable, the proportion of entrepreneurs in the society. The intervening mechanism involves business firms and their constituent occupations. This is the boundary structure. These occupations, McClelland explains, attract people with high n-achievement because they offer a field of risk-taking activity. Risk-taking activity is the boundary process. Thus, the needs of the n-achievers to take risks

[14] New York: Harper and Bros., 1958.

[15] New York: Jewish Publication Society (Meridian Books), 1960 (first published by Harper and Bros., 1947).

[16] Abridgment of Volumes 1–10, in two volumes, D. C. Somervell (ed.). Vols. 1–6, 1947; Vols. 7–10, 1957 (New York: Oxford University Press).

[17] Bollingen Series XLIII, trans. Franz Rosenthal (3 vols.: New York: Pantheon Books, 1958).

and the requirement of an occupational role, that its
occupants take risks, are meshed in this structure. The
structure "transforms" individual motivation into social
role behavior by providing a channel through which
motivation may be invested in a particular institutional
sphere.

In the above example the psychological factor is the
independent variable. The same type of transformation problem occurs when the direction of attention is
reversed and personality appears as a dependent variable. McClelland argues that the psychological characteristic of "other directedness" is positively correlated with economic development of a society. In this
statement "other directedness" is treated as the independent variable. "Other directedness" itself, however,
is a result of another economic factor, investment in
centralized employment rather than in cottage indus-
tries. "Other directedness" is the dependent variable.
McClelland explains that investment in centralized employment draws individuals out of their homes and into
the factory. There they come under the influence of the
opinions of fellow workers, and are easier to reach by
the mass media. They lose traditional particularistic
value patterns based on family and accept new univer-
salistic value patterns based on wage contracts. The
boundary structure is the factory. The boundary process is an interactive one, a form of adult socialization.
The independent economic variable, investment, creates the structure which provides the locus for the
processes which generate the psychological variable of
"other directedness."

In both of the McClelland examples, the boundary
structure was constituted by the social subsystem of
one of the two variables. Toynbee gives an example of
a statement in which the first variable is psychological

and the last is in the integrative social subsystem, while the intervening mechanism is in yet another social subsystem, the polity. Leaders, says Toynbee, infest themselves with the hypnotism they have induced in their followers and, as a result, lose initiative and cease to lead. This is a psychological self-attitude which has social consequences. Their tenure of power then becomes an abuse. The rank and file mutiny, and the leaders seek to restore order by drastic action. When the proletariat has mutinied or seceded and leaders have degenerated into a dominant minority, the civilization is disintegrating. The schism and subsequent disintegration is a disturbance in the integrative social subsystem. The boundary structure between the personality attribute and the socially integrative system consists of the power relation between leaders and followers, a problem of the polity. The boundary process is a negative one, the failure of role performance on the part of leaders. Power shifts in such a way that a problem of order, an integrative problem, is created. The transforming context is institutional and the process is interactive.

The mediating structure need not be a social institution or organization, nor need the process be interactive. When it is not, however, the direction of the transformation remains socially indeterminate. Toynbee describes creative individuals as having a need to transfigure their fellow men into fellow creators. This is a personality variable. In so doing, they may make life intolerable for some of their fellows. In response to this intolerable situation some of their fellows generate a changed society. A vague picture of the intervening mechanism is given. Tension is built up in members of society and this serves to motivate them to change society. Without specification of the institutional strucure and without specification of that interactive process involved in the tension reduction, there is no guarantee that the tension will be reduced by changing society rather than simply drawn off, say, by circuses.

Pattern maintenance or tension management processes may constitute the mediating mechanisms between personality and society. If this noninteractive subsystem is appealed to alone, the transformation remains socially indeterminate. However, the pattern maintenance-tension management subsystem has overlapping boundaries with—that is, serves as a cultural or motivational resource for—each of the three interactive systems. Consequently, it may operate through their interactive structures as a locus of personality-society transformation. Erikson shows how a personality variable is ramified into a political variable by virtue of a resonant response on the part of others. Erikson interprets the incident of Luther falling dumb in church as a reflection of Luther's need to say what is most worth saying in his native tongue. Partly in response to this language need, Luther translated the New Testament into German. The translation was an individual product but was done during a time of general verbal renaissance. Many people were anxious to reaffirm their identities in their native tongues. Luther's translation met this need and enjoyed audience response. By virtue of being read, it contributed to the cultivation of national vernaculars, an aspect of the growing nationalism. Thus, an individual personality variable, the need to speak in the vernacular, is correlated with a change in political culture, growing nationalism. The mediating process was the dialogue between an author and an audience—an educative process, part of the pattern maintenance system. The boundary structures, however, are religious and political institutions. There are two steps in the transformation. In the interactive context of the religious institution, a matching of Luther's motive with the motives of many others ramifies or amplifies the motive resonantly into a social factor. Then the social-religious variable is transformed into a social-political variable across the pattern maintenance boundary constituted by the common language, an aspect of nationalism.

McClelland provides an example in which a shared pattern maintenance boundary is the locus of a similar two-step transformation but from an independent social to a dependent personality variable. The previous example showed the pattern maintenance boundary in its function as a symbolic resource. The allocation of personnel in a society is also a pattern maintenance function. In McClelland's case it is this function as a resource for social personnel that is appealed to as a mediating mechanism. McClelland states that wars, an aspect of the polity, raise the level of n-achievement, an individual personality variable. The removal of authoritarian fathers from families is the linking explanation. (This proposition rests on another which states that sons have lower n-achievement when they are dominated by authoritarian fathers.) "Father" and "soldier" are two elements in the status sets of the same individuals. From the viewpoint of a social system, the problem is one of allocation of personnel among institutions. Personnel traverse the shared pattern maintenance boundary from the family to the polity. A political event thus becomes a family one. This is the first step in the transformation. Within the family, father-son socialization is the mediating process which transforms an attribute of family structure into an attribute of personality, n-achievement. The fact that many families are subjected to the same exigency allows McClelland to aggregate the effect and treat it as a characteristic of a collective.

Loops: A special case of an interdisciplinary statement is that in which the first and last variables are in the same system but the mediating mechanism called upon to explain their association is in another system or subsystem. Such statements may be called "loops." An example from Erikson shows how two types of belief, personality variables, are mediated by a social system variable. In discussing the problem of Luther's indoctrination with a new set of values in a monastic setting, he argues that former values are disengaged from intentions and aspirations through a social, spatial arrangement and temporal routine which isolates the individual. This arrangement narrows his sensory supply and blocks his sexual and aggressive drives. New convictions may then be offered and his new requirement will attach itself to a new world image. The structure intervening between the old and new beliefs is defined only by the spatial and temporal conditions and not limited to a specific institutional framework, though it is a monastery in this particular case. Blocking both the usual input and output of the psychic structure, then controlling available cognitive input so that the internal motivational energy has no recourse but to cathect the presented values or ideology, constitutes the mediating process.

Missing Links: When mediating mechanisms are not clearly specified, we lack a subjective sense that we "understand" the proposition. "Understanding" is related to the "how" as well as the "what" of a proposition. Moreover, without an intervening link, there is no way of ensuring that the correlation is not spurious. A statement of Erikson illustrates the problem of a missing link. Youths who feel estranged from certain social patterns sometimes force themselves, at the price of isolation, to insist on original ways of meeting existential problems. This leads to societal rejuvenation. The first variable is the feeling of estrangement; problem solving is the intervening process. Externally oriented action based on the solutions would not assure social regeneration, a social system outcome. This psychological occurrence might be isolated from a social context. The transformation from personality to social system requires an institutional context, some social locus for the problem-solving activity so that it may become socially relevant. Appeal to an aggregative principle is a weak, because indeterminate, substitute for an institutional context. A number of youths, perhaps due to a common structural situation, may arrive at common solutions and so have an impact on the social system. The weakness, however, is that sheer increase in numbers of parallel acts does not make them *social* acts, as is illustrated by the common example of many people opening their umbrellas in response to rain. We still need a context of interaction to explain how they come to work in concert.

Quasi-Interdisciplinary Statements: Some statements look interdisciplinary but, upon closer examination, turn out to be intradisciplinary. Erikson, for example, points out that Luther's father, a peasant miner, migrated and encouraged Luther to aspire to the managerial class. Luther became ambivalent about his ancestral identity and, as a consequence, his peasant background functioned as a negative identity. In later life he promoted the ruthless extermination of rebellious peasants. The first variable, migration from one to another part of the social structure, refers to the behavior of an individual and enters the statement as a source of a personal image. The intervening variable of Luther's ambivalence about his identity is a personality concept. Luther's promoting the extermination of the peasants is also an individual act, although its consequences may be social. By specifying social conditions that led others to follow Luther's behest and provided the means for turning individual motivation into collective behavior, a collective variable would be derived. Thus, Erikson's statement does not link personality and society (Luther's ambivalence with a repressive war against the peasants), but instead is a psychological statement about the sources of an identity and a personal act motivated by a characteristic of that identity.

LINKING SOCIAL SUBSYSTEMS

Statements that link two subsystems of the social system are also interdisciplinary but in a sense different from those linking personality and social system. In the latter case, the problem is to move from attributes of an individual to those that characterize a collective. All of the social subsystems refer to attributes of a collective but differ in the nature of the attributes. Mediating structures also play a part here.

Two social subsystems may be mediated by the personality participating in both. McClelland restates a well-known thesis of Max Weber's connecting the Protestant Reformation and the rise of the entrepreneurial spirit. This statement relates the cultural aspect of religion, the Protestant *ethic*, with the cultural aspect of the economy, the *spirit* of capitalism. As an intervening mechanism, McClelland discusses the impact of religious, ideological change on child-rearing patterns.

The Protestant home, valuing accomplishment and effort, produces more individuals with high n-achievement. When these individuals participate in the economy they promote the spirit of capitalism. The boundary structure is the family and the boundary process is socialization. Religious cultural input provides interactive norms. When family members interact according to these norms, the n-achieving personality is the outcome. N-achievers transfer the same types of norms to their economic roles.

The boundary mechanism may be a condition antecedent to the independent variable. Toynbee says that industrialism, when it emerged within the parochial state, generated the twin enormities of political and economic nationalism. He speaks of economic nationalism as a perversion of industrialism working within the constricting bonds of the parochial state. The parochial state is the institutional structure in which economic factors are transformed into a political-economic hybrid called economic nationalism.

Forged Link: An interesting case of the interdisciplinary statement is that in which the mediating structure comes into existence by virtue of the interaction of the independent and dependent variables. This may be described as a forged link. Toynbee says that when two civilizations have been in contact and one is in the process of being absorbed into the other, an intelligentsia emerges. First, military officers of the subordinated society learn the domineering society's art of war; then diplomatists are trained to negotiate; later merchants emerge to advance trade between them and schoolmasters appear to interpret one culture to the other. These groups are a class of liaison officers and constitute the intelligentsia. We begin with a problem in the adaptive system regarding the relation between two civilizations. As they become societies within the same civilization, the problem of their relation becomes one of system integration. The boundary is crossed in several institutional contexts. There is concrete interaction: soldiers interact in the sphere of power; merchants interact around the economy; schoolmasters interact around the cultural system. A new class with an integrative function emerges from this interaction.

Loops: Personality "loops" were discussed above. Loops also occur in statements relating two social subsystems. Toynbee observes that it is uncommon for the same "creative" minority to give creative responses to two or more successive challenges. The first and second responses to challenges are the two ends of the loop. Toynbee reasons that a creative response of a minority to a challenge places it in a position of power. Those who occupy such a position become infatuated with the past and therefore passive. Challenged a second time, they fail to respond creatively. The intervening mechanism involves the polity, especially the position of certain individuals in the power structure. Conditions of their positions affect their personalities. Individuals in power receive satisfactions that encourage them to fixate on past and present and to resist structural change. Passivity becomes a personality characteristic of those who are inhibited from acting. They become incapable of responding creatively to a later challenge. Through ramification in many personalities this individual incapacity becomes a social inability to respond.

An example of a loop in which the mediating link is forged is given by Toynbee. During transmarine migration by the Greeks, individuals emigrate from a polity based on kinship ties. They form ships' companies and learn to co-operate on the basis of contract. When later they are obliged to hold a strip of coast against a hostile hinterland and establish Greek overseas settlements, this form of polity based on contract tends to continue. Thus the proposition begins and ends with a polity variable, but the mediating mechanism involves the emergence of transitional collectivities in which new forms of relationships are evolved. The mediating mechanisms are in the integrative subsystem.

Ibn Khaldun provides another example of a loop within a social system. When royal authority claims all glory for itself (and not as the common property of the group), there is a tendency to treat others severely, control them and prevent them from owning property. Those so treated become dispirited and come to venerate humbleness. As a result, they think of military service in terms of the allowances they receive. But individuals would not hire themselves out to sacrifice their lives. Consequently, "group feeling" decays and the dynasty progresses toward weakness. The first variable refers to the allocation of power and prestige —royal authority and its claims to glory; the last refers to the decline of the power holders—the progress of the dynasty toward weakness. Both are in the polity. The mediating mechanisms are, however, in other systems. The maldistribution of rewards that creates a need for more forceful social control is an integrative problem. This type of social control eliminates popular initiative and reduces group commitment. When this is widespread, "group feeling" declines and the dynasty that depends on it declines. This is a tension management problem, the loss of a motivational resource of the social system, that has consequences for the polity with which it shares a boundary.

Multi-Step Transformation: In discussing personality-society propositions, two-step transformations were found, as, for example, in the proposition relating Luther's need to speak in the vernacular and the growth of nationalism. The above example from Ibn Khaldun involves both the integrative and tension management systems as intervening mechanisms. Following is an example which appears to involve several mediating mechanisms linking two subsystems. In reality, these are the same subsystems and a loop is involved. Toynbee says that militarism is the most common cause of the breakdown of civilizations. The first tendency is to see this as a relation between a political ideology and system integration. For Toynbee, however, the civilization constitutes the social system and the societies are units in the system. Militarism, therefore, is a principle of order, of conflict, between the units of the system. It is thus an integrative ideological problem. Disintegration of the civilization is possible, Toynbee explains, because militarism causes the local states, which the society articulates, to collide with one another in destructive fratricidal conflicts. This represents the breakdown of system integration. The statement, thus far, is intrasystemic from the viewpoint of the civilization. The second basis for the breakdown is that each entire society intensifies the conflict. This entails the depletion of economic material and human resources without which the society cannot adapt to its environment. Here we have, in effect, a loop in which two integrative issues are linked through the economy.

The boundary mechanism may be quite complex. For example, Ibn Khaldun notes that a nation that has been defeated and comes under the rule of another nation, a political variable, will quickly perish, an integrative variable. When they lose control of their own affairs, people become apathetic. Hopelessness and apathy cause population decrease. Thus, a loss of motivational resource, a tension management problem, ensues from the change in the polity. Business activity comes to a halt, and people are unable to defend themselves. Adaptive and goal attainment problems ensue, with the result that the nation perishes. Pattern maintenance, adaptive and goal attainment structures have all been involved in the transformation of an event in the polity to one in the integrative subsystem.

Schumpeter gives an example of economic forces producing a political result by crossing the pattern maintenance boundary, but drawing upon several aspects of pattern maintenance and tension management. The capitalist process, an event in the economy, encourages the rationalization of behavior, a consequence for the personality. From Schumpeter's point of view, rational orientations are ramified through the system, a pattern maintenance issue. They drive out romantic ideas. When these factors are combined with a pre-existent condition, a sense of duty, utilitarian ideas of betterment are the result. Again, this is a pattern maintenance issue. When combined with a motivational element, the capitalist enthusiasm for efficiency, such ideas stimulate the "will" for social legislation. A tension management event underlies social legislation, an event in the polity. The transformation from the economic to the political was made solely with reference to pattern maintenance and tension management. Ordinarily, reference to the pattern maintenance system also leaves the transformation indeterminate. It may be satisfactory here because the values and motives direct behavior in specific interaction systems.

Missing Links: Schumpeter provides an example of a statement relating family and the economy in which a link appears to be missing. He argues that the bourgeoisie are not concerned with consumption but with accumulation. Accumulation is a way of providing for future generations, a family motive. With the decline of the bourgeois family, the businessman's time horizon shrinks to his life expectation and he drifts into an anti-conservative frame of mind. This then decomposes capitalism from within by depriving the economic system of its needed resources. The mediating mechanism is the anti-conservative frame of mind. For this to actually affect the economy it would have to be translated into an interactive factor. Failure to cite this leaves a gap.

Rise and Fall of Subsystems: A special case of an interdisciplinary statement is that which accounts for the differentiation of two systems from one another. Baron, discussing the polity of the new Protestant church, notes that its hierarchy is not under extra-territorial government and there is no sacramental distinction between the laymen and the clergy. These conditions open the road to an influx of lay, or predominantly national, ideologies. The outcome is lay control, that is, control by state organs. Thus religion and state are differentiated in the process. From the point of view of the broad society there has been a change in its integrative subsystem; a new set of relations between religious and national institutions has evolved. The allocation of personnel and ideology, a shared pattern maintenance boundary, mediates here.

An example of the blurring of system boundaries is

Baron's statement of the relation between religious pietism—treated as an ethic or ideology and so part of the pattern maintenance system—and subsequent all-German nationalism, an aspect of the polity. The intervening argument is that pietism taught enthusiasm and mystic union with the Creator, thus setting the pattern for national enthusiasm and the irrationalism of all-German nationalists. Thus pietism fostered all-German nationalism. Religion and nationalism affect one another by sharing the same pattern maintenance boundary.

SUMMATION

The "total study" of a "total society" involves linking concepts belonging to different theoretical networks. The simplest case is that of the bi-disciplinary statement. A "good" bi-disciplinary statement will involve two terms each referring to a distinct theoretical system—for example, one referring to the personality and the other to the social system; or to distinct subsystems —for example, one referring to the polity and the other to the economy. The statement will also cite a mechanism that mediates the events in these two systems. Usually the mechanism consists of an interactive process within a specified social structure. The function of the mechanism is to transform an event in one system into an event in another system. If no mechanism is cited, the asserted co-occurrence of events remains indeterminate. The mechanism may be antecedent to the independent event, or forged by the interaction of the independent and dependent events or be in a third system or subsystem that shares a boundary with both the dependent and independent events. A special case is that of the loop in which the independent and dependent events are two states of the same system. A mechanism in another system may be called upon to explain the change of state.

JAMES S. COLEMAN

GAME MODELS OF ECONOMIC AND POLITICAL SYSTEMS

INTRODUCTION

I shall attempt here to describe the functioning of a social system in a way most useful for understanding social and political change within that system. I shall not, however, approach the problem of change directly. Instead, I shall try to model the functioning of the system first and afterward to examine the processes through which change takes place. Obviously, such an enterprise is in its infancy. I propose, then, to discuss not its results, but the strategy for its execution.

This strategy is not a common one in the development of social theory; yet I believe it will be very productive. It consists of two stages: first, the development of a game to mirror the dominant processes in the system; second, the development of a theory that describes symbolically the functioning of the game.

The use of a game as a way station between vague ideas and formal theory seems to be particularly appropriate for the kind of social theory I find most appealing. The nature of such a theory is that it begins with rational actors about whom one can assume nothing more than that each will act in his own interest. Thus many elements taken as given in certain social theories become problematic: the existence of norms, the phenomenon of identification or empathy, the investment of one's self in collective goals, and so on.

The theorist who starts only with the assumption that self-interest motivates action, faces the difficult task of fashioning a viable system from it. In contrast with most other starting points in social theory, the very structure of the system itself is problematic.

This kind of social theory has some important elements in common with games. Perhaps most important is that each player in a game is motivated to win, and the game or the social system must function as a by-product of the diverse goals of individual wills. To construct a game that simulates the functioning of a social system, one must create a kind of interdependence among the players, so that, despite the diversity and possible conflict of goals, the game is viable, the system functions. Moreover, the system thus created must have some isomorphism with the social system it is designed to simulate.

Once this has been done, the development of an abstract theory becomes much simpler than before. For in constructing a game, one must be precise about the resources with which each player begins, and how he may use them to further his ends. The construction of a theory then requires the appropriate formal abstractions for the resources (for example, in terms of certain kinds of quantities), and for the activities engaged in by the players (for example, mathematical or computer operations upon the quantities).

THE GAME

I shall describe two games. Both take as their base a system of interdependent economic activities. A different system of activities might have been taken as the base; however, my selection of the economic system reflects a belief that these are the most fundamental in a model that is ultimately concerned with political processes.

The economic system is a simple one. It consists of four kinds of economic activities: extraction (mining), manufacturing, agriculture, labor.

There are four kinds of players: a mine owner, a manufacturer, farmers, and workers. The system of production is described by the table below, and by tables B, C, D, and E, which are used in the game described in the Appendix to this chapter.

Inputs	Process	Outputs
Workers' labor Manufactured goods	Mining	Raw materials
Raw materials Workers' labor Manufactured goods	Manufacturing	Manufactured goods
Farmers' labor Manufactured goods Weather	Farming	Food
Manufactured goods Food	Consumption	Labor

The consumption schedule is identical for all players. All must consume in each time period a certain minimum quantity of food and a certain minimum quantity of manufactured goods. All consumption above these minima provides satisfaction according to a schedule of decreasing marginal satisfaction. Tables F and G, used in the game, show these schedules of satisfaction. In addition, workers and farmers incur negative satisfaction for their hours of labor, as indicated in Table A.

A few other conditions exist. For example, food is perishable after one time period. Initial conditions are set to allow production to begin (that is, an initial distribution of money and manufactured goods), and play proceeds. (The rules of the game are given as an appendix.)

No prices are fixed, and there is no external constraint on the system. The only inputs from the environment are those raw materials, manufactured goods, and food created in the production process. The only outputs to the environment are those raw materials, manufactured goods, and food utilized in the production process or consumed.

Obviously, little can be inferred from such a simple game about the functioning of systems it is designed to simulate. However, one important step toward the goal has been taken: a system of interdependence has been established that functions, and does not go wild. (Although systematic experimentation with the game remains to be carried out, a great deal of play has demonstrated that the system does function.) The importance of such a step has not generally been recognized, perhaps because social scientists have been so concerned with the detail of social systems that they have overlooked the necessity for putting the system together again. In any case, once such a system has been constructed, it can serve as the core of a vastly extended one that embodies detail.

The first step in such elaboration is the development of a public sector of the economy. The game described above is predicated on a very simple system that produces only private goods, one with no collective decisions or collective actions whatsoever. Yet all societies take certain actions as a collectivity. That is to say, all societies have some kind of government. Thus this first very important elaboration is incorporated in the second game.

In the second game, a legislature of five members is elected by popular vote every two years (with each time period representing a year). Each legislator continues to fill one of the economic roles in the society. The function of the legislature is threefold: a) to pass bills that provide public services (police, roads, and education) that give satisfaction (differentially) to the various actors; b) to levy a tax to pay for the public services provided; and c) to change the rules of the game in whatever way they see fit. The first two actions are passed by majority vote; the last requires unanimity. Anyone may run for office. Table H, I, and J show the conditions under which each of the three public services operates, and the satisfactions derived from each by each type of player. (For each service, the legislature appoints a non-legislator [unpaid] to carry out hiring and buying, subject to the funds appropriated by the legislature for that public service.)

Obviously, such a simple governing mechanism does not simulate reality. Importantly, however, it has supplemented a system of economic interdependence with a procedure for collective decisions. This comes a step closer to encompassing those elements most crucial for studying social and political change. Although it contains these processes in extremely simple forms, this defect may not be so critical as one would at first suppose.

THE THEORY

A game, like the reality it attempts to simulate, must be concrete, whereas the theory must consist of abstract elements. Fortunately, if the game is fruitful, relative to the theory of interest, it will have already accounted for some portion of the abstraction, making the next step a simpler one. The discussion below indicates how this occurs in the present case.

Let us assume a rough form the theory will take. First, there are activities, such as production of raw materials, production of food, election of legislators, and passage of laws. For simplicity at the outset, let us consider only economic production. We can specify two things about the relationship of each activity to the actors: which actor has direct control over it, and the nature of consumption interest each actor has in its product. That is, we can describe each activity in terms of the distribution of control over it, and in terms of the distribution of final consumption interests in its products. Conversely, we can describe each actor in terms of the distribution of his control over activities, and in terms of the distribution of his interests in the outputs from various activities. (The distribution of interests can be conceived much like a marginal utility: how an additional unit of the good affects the degree of his satisfaction.)

Each kind of information may be thought of as a matrix, with actors as rows and activities as columns. Connecting these two matrices is a third matrix, deriving from the technology of the economic system. This is an input-output matrix, which relates the input in certain activities to the output in others. In this simplified model, the chain of production and consumption thus consists of three points: control by actors of the activities that constitute the factors of production; intermediate consumption of these factors in the production of others; and specific interests of individuals in the final consumption of each of the products of these activities.

The set of activities not described by these matrices are those activities that "adjust" the system: the exchange processes that go on either in a market or in bargaining. These processes are dictated by the matrix of intermediate consumption and the matrix of final consumption or interests. The principle of economic rationality applied to this situation states that each actor will attempt to maximize his control of those activities whose products interest him most, i.e., those that are of most marginal utility to him.

Now if we digress briefly to consider a pure legislative system, we may describe it in identical terms, lacking only the intermediate input-output matrix. Consider a set of activities under control of the legislature. Essentially, they are "issues" on which that body can take action in one direction or another. The only difference between the legislative and the economic model is that the structure of control over these activities is equally distributed (in a simple homogeneous legislature) over all legislators. Thus this matrix of control is one with equal entries in all cells.

As in the economic system, there is a matrix of interests in each of these activities, showing the marginal utility to each legislator of an increment (in a given direction) of each of these activities. In an ideally functioning legislature these interests reflect the interests of constituents, who vote according to the decisions made by the legislature with regard to those matters of greatest marginal utility to him. In actual legislatures, other sources of interest to the legislators exist, such as personal economic gain. However, these variations are irrelevant to this simple system.

The matrix of interests, in contrast to the matrix of control, will show a very uneven distribution: some legislators will have strong interests in certain activities (i.e., issues); others will have strong interests in different activities.

The principle of economic rationality, applied to the legislature, is identical to that applied to the economic system. Each actor will attempt to maximize his control of those activities that interest him most. He can utilize a method he employs within the economic system, namely, exchange of control over those activities that interest him least for control over those activities that interest him most. The principal exchange is an exchange of votes; i.e., agreements to cast one's vote on issue A in a specified way in return for a comparable concession by another actor. Other sources of control, such as that of the order of legislation, also affect such exchange processes.

There are two major differences between the legislative system and the economic system, as I have described them. The first is the difference between collective control and individual control. The second difference is found in the distribution of control and interests. In the legislative system, the distribution of control is even, and the distribution of interests is uneven. Consequently, actors carry out exchanges in such a way as to make their distribution of control over activities more uneven, to match their interests. In the economic system I have described, exactly the reverse is true. The distribution of interests (in final consumption) is even, but the distribution of control is very uneven. Consequently, the exchanges will be such as to even out the distribution of control over the products of activities (i.e., goods), again to match the distribution of interests.

The systems I have described above are a rudimentary formulation. Obviously they are only initial steps toward an adequate description of the functioning of a political system in the context of a given economic one. Their chief virtue is that they cast both systems into the same conceptual terms, thus beginning the incorporation of the two into a single conceptual system.

APPENDIX

Rules for Economic System Game

PLAYERS
1. One mine owner
2. One manufacturer
3. Four workers
4. Three farmers

PLAY
1. Manufacturer and miner begin the game with $450 each. Farmers begin with $100, and workers with $50.
2. At beginning of play, miner begins with 50 units of manufactured goods, manufacturer with 20 and each farmer with 15.
3. Hiring is done on an open-market basis by mine owner and manufacturer. Mine owner and manufacturer offer wages; workers may accept or refuse. Workers are hired for hourly wages, in increments of 5. Workers are paid when hired.
4. Mine owner calculates his production, and offers his raw materials to manufacturer at whatever price he desires. Manufacturer and miner agree on a price. (If they do not agree, they will lose the game to farmers and workers, for they must pay wages for agreed-upon times at agreed-upon rates, and calculation of score as indicated below will make them losers.)
5. Manufacturer now calculates his production, depending on his labor, raw materials and manufactured goods. Production is at level indicated by lowest of these items. (Same is true of miner's pro-

duction.) If raw materials remain, they may be stored at a cost of .5 hours of labor per unit of raw materials, subtracted from his current or next year's labor supply. After the first round, the miner or manufacturer can also store manufactured goods, at a cost of .3 units of labor for each unit of manufactured good, subtracted from his current or next year's labor supply.

6. In the meantime, the farmers are each deciding (independently) how much manufactured goods and how many hours of their own labor to invest in food production. By use of a die to represent weather, this input is then translated into food produced. Farmers must keep a record of their units of (negative) satisfaction incurred in this production. Farmer may sell food on an open market to anyone as soon as he produces it.

7. Any manufactured goods remaining in the hands of manufacturer or bought by a mine can be stored at a cost of .3 hours of labor per unit. Storage charges are calculated only on those goods not used as input to the production process in the next round. Food is perishable and cannot be stored beyond a single period, although costs for storage are 0 for that single period of storage. The farmer can store manufactured goods at the same labor costs (for his own labor) as the manufacturer and miner. The labor costs are directly accountable in terms of the dissatisfaction this labor produces (see Table A).

8. The game continues for an indeterminate number of rounds. Total scores are determined by adding together the satisfaction scores (including the negative satisfactions) received throughout the game for consumption (and also, for farmers and workers, dissatisfaction incurred in labor). One point is subtracted from total score for every dollar held at the game's beginning, and one point is added to it for every dollar held at the end. Raw materials and

manufactured goods stored at end of game do not count in the scoring.

ADDITIONAL RULES FOR PUBLIC GOODS

1. At the end of first round of play, a legislature of five members is elected by popular vote, with each player having five votes, which he can use to vote for one or more candidates, up to five.
2. At the end of the second round, the legislature meets and determines how much of each of the public goods to purchase through passage of bills by majority vote. After such bills have been passed, the total funds required are calculated by the legislature, and a tax bill is passed. Taxation may treat players differentially by wealth, income, or occupation, or may tax all the same amount. The legislature appoints commissioners for each of the public goods, and a tax collector. Each of these players performs this role in addition to his private economic activity during the next two rounds of play. Any bills to change the rules of the game may be entertained by the legislature.
3. At the end of the next round of play (round 4) and on even-numbered rounds thereafter, a legislative election is held, and any non-legislator can propose to run against any of the five incumbents. If unopposed, the existing legislator remains.
4. The legislature meets at the end of each odd-numbered round, to carry out activities described in (2) above.

TABLE A

Units of satisfaction (negative) incurred by farmers per hour of own labor expended

Hours of labor:	10	20	30	40	50	60	70	80	90	100	100+
Units of satisfaction:	0	0	−1	−3	−6	−10	−15	−21	−28	−36	−00

TABLE B

*Units of effective input per hours of labor
and units of manufactured goods expended*

		HOURS OF LABOR									
		10	20	30	40	50	60	70	80	90	100
Units of	5	1	1	2	2	3	3	4	4	5	5
manufactured goods	10	1	2	2	3	4	4	4	5	5	5
	15	1	2	2	3	4	6	6	6	7	7
	20	1	2	3	4	5	6	7	8	8	9
	25	2	2	3	4	5	6	7	8	9	10

TABLE C

*Units of food output per unit of effective input
as affected by weather*

		UNITS OF EFFECTIVE INPUT									
		1	2	3	4	5	6	7	8	9	10
Outcome of die	1	24	27	30	33	36	39	42	45	48	51
	2	27	30	33	36	39	42	45	48	51	54
	3	30	33	36	39	42	45	48	51	54	57
	4	33	36	39	42	45	48	51	54	57	60
	5	36	39	42	45	48	51	54	57	60	63
	6	39	42	45	48	51	54	57	60	63	66

TABLE D

*Manufacturer's production per unit of raw materials,
input manufactured goods, and hours of labor*

UNITS OF RAW MATERIALS	UNITS OF MANUFACTURED GOODS	HOURS OF LABOR	PRODUCTION OF OUTPUT IN UNITS MANUFACTURED GOODS
20	20	20	100
28	20	30	140
36	20	40	180
44	20	50	220
50	20	60	250
56	20	70	280
60	20	80	300
64	20	90	320
68	20	100	340
72	20	110	360
74	20	120	370

TABLE E

*Units of mine production per unit input of
labor and manufactured goods*

MANUFACTURED GOODS	HOURS OF LABOR	UNITS MINED
10	20	10
15	30	20
20	40	30
26	50	40
32	60	50
39	75	60
46	90	70
54	105	80
62	120	90
71	140	100
81	160	110

TABLE F   TABLE G

Satisfaction levels from consumption

MANUFACTURED GOODS		FOOD	
CONSUMP-TION	SATIS-FACTION	CONSUMP-TION	SATIS-FACTION
below 10	—	below 10	—
10	6	10	0
11	12	11	10
12	17	12	19
13	22	13	27
14	26	14	34
15	30	15	40
16	33	16	45
17	36	17	49
18	38	18	52
19	40	19	54
20	41	20	55
21	42	over 20	55
over 21	42		

TABLE H

Road expenditures

	INPUTS			SATISFACTION TO:		
LABOR	MANU-FACTURED GOODS	MINE OWNER	MANU-FACTURER	FARMERS	WORKERS
0	0	—	−50	—	0
10	5	0	0	0	0
20	10	6	3	6	1
30	15	12	6	12	2
40	20	17	9	17	3
50	25	22	11	22	3
60	30	26	13	26	3
70	35	30	14	30	4
80	40	33	14	33	4
90	45	36	15	36	4
100	50	38	15	38	4
110	55	40	15	40	4
120	60	41	15	41	4
over 120	over 60	41	15	41	4

TABLE I

Education

	INPUTS			SATISFACTION TO:		
LABOR	MANU-FACTURED GOODS	MINE OWNER	MANU-FACTURER	FARMERS	WORKERS
0	0	0	0	−25	−50
10	5	0	0	0	0
20	5	1	1	3	6
30	10	2	2	6	12
40	10	3	3	9	17
50	15	3	3	11	22
60	15	3	3	13	26
70	20	4	4	14	30
80	20	4	4	14	33
90	28	4	4	15	36
100	28	4	4	15	38
110	30	4	4	15	40
120	30	4	4	15	41
over 120	over 30	4	4	15	41

TABLE J

Police

INPUTS		SATISFACTION TO:			
LABOR	MANU-FACTURED GOODS	MINE OWNER	MANU-FACTURER	FARMERS	WORKERS
0	0	−50	—	0	0
5	10	0	0	0	0
10	20	3	6	1	3
15	30	6	12	2	6
20	40	9	17	3	9
25	50	11	22	3	11
30	60	13	26	3	13
35	70	14	30	4	14
40	80	14	33	4	14
45	90	15	36	4	15
50	100	15	38	4	15
55	110	15	40	4	15
60	120	15	41	4	15
over 60	over 120	15	41	4	15

ITHIEL DE SOLA POOL

COMPUTER SIMULATIONS OF
TOTAL SOCIETIES

The study of total societies is not novel. At least since
Herodotus it has been a favorite pursuit of mankind.
Historians and anthropologists, both of whom have engaged in this pursuit, have much to teach us about
what can be done, how it should be done, and what
cannot be done.

One of the first lessons of historiography is that
while it is possible to study a total society, it is not
possible to study a total society totally. There is no
such thing as a complete description of even the smallest event. The job of the historian is to select. Out of
the infinite complexity of reality he reports some few
aspects which seem to him important, illustrative, indicative. Only a most naïve historian believes that
these are "the facts." They are some facts, and a different historian with a different purpose and a different
perspective might have chosen different facts.

Another key insight of both anthropologists and historians is that these myriad events are not independent
or equally influential. Cultures have a certain unity.
They are coherent. There are "patterns of culture." If
one knows how a culture treats violence between siblings and between siblings and parents, one is likely
to be able to guess how it treats violence among neighbors and citizens. A culture is not a random series of
folkways and mores.

Out of these two insights—that one can never describe more than a small sample of the events that constitute a society and that these events are not all of equal significance, some being more indicative of fundamental patterns than others—grow many of the theses presented over the past century about how to study societies. However, these two propositions constitute an incomplete set of equations, an indeterminate system. They tell us something of great importance about how to describe a society, but they do not tell us enough to decide exactly what facts to include in a description of a total society. They do help us to distinguish profound from shallow work, good descriptions of societies from bad ones, for they provide some of the necessary criteria of criticism. But while such propositions do enable us to distinguish good work from bad work, they are inadequate to enable us to choose among good works.

There are an infinite number of alternative good, profound, sophisticated descriptions of the same society. There is no limit to the number of books that could be written about the United States with different selections of data to demonstrate the values we have, the social structure, the prevailing beliefs and expectations, the traditions, the customs, etc.

An incomplete system is never satisfactory to a scholar. It is always an invitation to find the other variables and relationships not yet identified, which enable one to come up with a unique solution. For a century and a half, historians and social scientists have proposed more specific rules for the description of total societies. We have been told that we should start by looking at the mode of production and that we will find all other human relations to be reflections of them. We have been told to look at early child training and that the character of the culture is fixed by that. We have been told that one can enumerate sets of values and then categorize the society according to its selection among them. All of these insights have proved fruitful in that they have identified important factors, i.e., factors with greater predictive powers than some others we might choose. But there is no consensus on any such grand scheme for the description of a total society.

I would go further: not only is there no consensus, there will be none. There is no reason to believe that after a hundred and fifty years of unsuccessful striving, anyone is going to come along now with a set of rules about the right way to describe a total society. The search for a body of theory that identifies which things are important and which things unimportant is likely to produce nothing but a rehash of familiar arguments from the past hundred years. The search for such theories of historical determination is a much over-worked topic in the social sciences in which the prospect of discovering anything new is very small indeed. The sophistication of the description of a total society by a historian or an anthropologist fifty years hence (except insofar as he is able to use new data collection and summarization tools) is likely to be no better than that of a Robert Lynd or a Ruth Benedict or a Karl Marx or a Max Weber.

I am sure that this essentially negative conclusion about the likely development of verbal macro-theories of society will not be shared by many of my colleagues. I will not try to argue the issue, however, since it is one of prediction, and concededly my pessimism is not a demonstrable conclusion. There will be little argument, however, with the statement that we are not very good at describing complex total societies rigorously and objectively, and that we have not made much progress in that in recent years.

From this consensus in discouragement arises an interest in simulation as a possible way of studying total societies. There is always a temptation to have exaggerated expectations for each new development in the social sciences. One such development which is indeed a major breakthrough for the analysis of complex systems is the technique of simulation. There is a natural inclination to feel that perhaps here at last we have a means for the study of total societies that will enable us to do what we have not so far been able to do, i.e., to find unique correct solutions. There is a tendency to believe that if only we can do a simulation of a society we will have achieved a complete, accurate representation about which we may say "this is the description of that society." There is some foundation for this view, although it is essentially incorrect.

A simulation is designed as an answer to the question of what would happen under some hypothetical future circumstances. One may simulate the effects of campaign strategies, or of marketing strategies, or of different organizational structures. In each case one is posing and trying to answer a "what if" question, to make a conditional prediction. Thus a simulation model must be sufficiently complex and the relationships within it sufficiently well defined to permit one to emerge with a specific prediction of the outcome under a specific hypothetical set of circumstances. (More accurately, if the model is stochastic, one must emerge with a specific prediction of the statistical distribution of a set of possible outcomes.) A simulation model therefore needs to be highly rigorous.

A simulation model may be contrasted with a typical *ceteris paribus* statement about variables taken pairwise, the kind of proposition of which most of social science consists. Typically if a social scientist says there is a tendency for Y to go one way if X goes a certain way, he makes it clear that he is not making a specific prediction of the value of Y because he is only singling out one of its determinants in a statement which is true only insofar as other things remain constant. The simulator, on the other hand, attempts to bring in all the variables that he considers to be important in determining the outcome, to state the relationships among them with such completeness that only one degree of freedom remains, and in that way to state what the actual outcome would be if a particular variable X were changed in a certain way.

That, however, does not mean that his model is the only valid model of the system that he is studying. A different model may be necessary to predict a different dependent variable in the same system. Indeed it is conceivable that two models would each predict the same dependent variable equally well. For example, to cite a familiar joke: one can measure the number of cows in a field either by counting the number of their heads or by counting the number of their legs and dividing by four. In the same way there may be many identically good and essentially substitutable indicators of a political or social fact. It may turn out that revolutions, for example, are equally well predicted by studying dissatisfaction of social classes or the accumulation of weapons in the hands of subversive organizations that are prepared to use them. If both conditions are necessary for a revolution and come about together then either one may provide an indicator in a simulation model as in any other social science procedure. Thus it is valid to say that a simulation of a total society, if successful, enables one to make specific predictions of outcomes but it is still not true that there is any one unique best simulation.

We have stated the essential requirement for a simulation to be that we can state the variables and their relations with sufficient precision to provide us with a determinate solution to a closed system. The system must provide a single definite prediction for each change that can be introduced in the independent variables. This degree of precision in outcome can be achieved in a number of ways, but one way or another there must be a decision rule that specifies what will happen to dependent variable Y when there is some specified hypothetical condition for each of the independent variables $X_1, X_2 \ldots X_n$.

Such decision rules can be of two kinds. They can either specify what the decision should be or they can specify who makes the decision. Thus a fundamental distinction among kinds of simulations is between mathematical or computer simulations on the one hand and human simulations (more often called games), on the other.

In the human simulation or game, a player is presented with a complex situation that has arisen out of the initial scenario and the previous moves of himself and other players. When it is his turn he makes a well-defined move; he takes into account all the circumstances, decides what would or should be done by the person or institution whose role he is playing. He thus provides a completely definite outcome to the complex conditions hypothetically proposed. The decision rule simply specifies who chooses that outcome. Since the outcome is definite such games are properly called simulations. Since over several plays of the games different outcomes may be chosen by different players in identical circumstances, such games are properly described as stochastic simulations, and the result of the analysis of the simulation is more accurately described as a measure of the distribution of possible outcomes than as a single outcome.

In this paper we shall not consider human games further. We turn our attention to those simulations where the decision rules specify the outcome rather than specifying the authoritative decision maker. Such simulations are formal models, usually mathematical, and usually so complex that they can in practice only be operated with the aid of a computer. Their essential character, however, is neither that they are quantitative nor that they are computer-operated but that the formal model is sufficiently well defined to give a specific outcome. There must be no extra degrees of freedom producing indeterminacy of the outcome.

That may in many instances be achieved only by way of a device that to some degree resembles human simulation more than it resembles a typical mathematical model, namely a Monte Carlo device. One or more of the decision rules of the simulation may be to select a random number. Where that is done there is still a definite outcome because the random number gets selected. However, it will not provide the same outcome every time. Thus once again the analysis of such a simulation yields information only about the statistical distribution of those outcomes rather than about a single inevitable outcome. Nonetheless such simulations fit our definition. In each run there is a determinate prediction for any given hypothetical set of circumstances.

I cannot think of any complex formal simulation model which is completely non-quantitative. In principle, however, there can surely be one. Let us consider as a near example a simulation of English speech. Let us imagine that we have programed a computer to start with a word, then to look up in a dictionary what grammatical part of speech it is, then to provide another word that, according to English grammar, can follow such a part of speech, then to provide another word that could follow such a pair, etc., until one has had the computer create a grammatical English sentence. This is not an example of a completely non-quantitative simulation, given the many words in the dictionary that can follow any other given word or series of words. A Monte Carlo device would have picked one of them by means of a random number. Nonetheless, the role of quantity is clearly very minimal in such a simulation. So this simulation may serve as an example to show that computers are devices for proceeding according to rigorous formal rules. They are not necessarily arithmetic machines.

These points have a good deal to do with whether a simulation of a total society is feasible or not. On the one hand when people pooh-pooh this possibility by saying that there are many crucially important non-quantitative things to be said in describing a total society, they are raising an illegitimate objection. The statement is true but it may be an argument for the value of computer simulation rather than against. If the qualitative statements made are at all rigorous they can be said in computer language just as well as in English. There is nothing unambiguous that cannot be said in a computer interpretable code. Joseph Weizenbaum has said, and with some merit, that the time is not far off when no social science theory that cannot be reduced to a computer model will be given any credence or respect because its non-reducibility can only mean its ambiguity. The problem then is not one of quantity versus quality, it is one of precision versus ambiguity.

So while the simulation of total societies is possible, both in their qualitative as well as quantitative aspects, let us not assume it is always a sensible thing to do. It is sensible only if our thinking is sufficiently advanced so that we can replace all ambiguous expressions by definite ones. For numerous problems that is not the case. To cite an example from the field of marketing, no one has come up with a good simulation of advertising effectiveness, although many people have tried. The problem is that the phrase "advertising effectiveness" is ambiguous. Is it to be measured in awareness of the product, in its image, or perhaps, most obviously, in sales? The trouble with sales as a measure, however, is that they are also dependent upon many other factors besides advertising such as distribution, consumer habits, etc. Thus a simulation in which the dependent variable is sales must be a simulation not only of advertising but of the entire marketing process. In such a simulation we can give the concept of advertising effectiveness a definite meaning in terms of sales but at the same time we find that we have to introduce into a total market model several other equally ambiguous and poorly defined variables. Our state of knowledge about the total system is such as to make the attempt to produce a simulation of advertising effectiveness a futile one. It is possible to produce simulations of the frequency of advertising exposures, it is possible to produce simulations of the learning and forgetting process as the result of exposure; these are well-defined problems (partially qualitative, partially quantitative); they are, however, only sub-problems of the larger one of defining advertising effectiveness. The larger one is one we are not yet ready for.

Do not conclude from this that total society simulations are impossible. It is not always true that larger problems are harder to represent than smaller ones. That would be true only for models that are reductionistic. If, in general, models of larger systems had to be based on models of their subsystems then no social model would be possible except on the basis of a biological model and no biological model except on the basis of a chemical model. Clearly social scientists reject this view.

In short, there is no *a priori* reason why total society simulations should be impossible. They are not ruled out by the qualitative character of much of our understanding of social processes; they are not ruled out by the complexity of the reality they represent, nor by the number of subsystems they encompass.

On the other hand, the skeptic about total society simulation is probably more often right than wrong because more often than not we lack sufficiently definite information about the facts and relationships in the particular system that we have chosen to represent to provide an effective simulation. As a practical matter, the way to go about deciding whether a problem is ready for computer simulation is to try to sketch out with pencil and paper the relationships among the variables to see how far we think we can state them in a rigorous manner. A flow chart is a commonly used device for representing such a set of relationships, as is a series of simultaneous equations. It may also be done in verbal form.

But having a flow diagram does not make the problem computerizable. That depends on whether the relationships so easy to represent by lines and boxes can be stated rigorously. If one feels that one can state enough of them rigorously so that implications of a non-obvious character probably follow, then it probably is worthwhile undertaking the intellectual task of formalizing these relationships into a computer model. If the propositions form only a loose web and few non-obvious results would follow from their interactions, then what is called for is not computer simulation but more work on the underlying pieces of theory, for a simulation is merely an expression of theories. If the propositions are rich, numerous, and interrelated but so vaguely stated that nothing definite can be said to follow, then again what is called for is not computer simulation but more work on the conceptualization of the theory.

Let me cite some examples of situations that lent themselves to simulation. In 1960 I engaged in a simulation of presidential campaign strategies. The basic body of theory represented in that simulation was extremely simple as simulations go. There were some dozen variables in the equations. Three or four general propositions interrelated them in rather simple form. These general propositions are known in the social sciences as the theory of cross-pressure and are presented in the Berelson-Lazarsfeld-McPhee volume *Voting*. In addition to these few variables and simple propositions, however, there were in the model a very large number of parameters which had to be rather accurately estimated for the model to work. The propositions had to do with such matters as the probability of a person switching his vote as a function of party affiliation and issue attitudes. The parameters also measured such things as the number of people who had a certain issue attitude or who had a certain party affiliation in a particular state. In this instance the simulation was worth undertaking and worked well because it happened that there was a large body of good data for measuring these many parameters. That body of data was the accumulated public opinion polls from the previous decade. They provided us with good measures of such matters as civil rights attitudes or the degree of anti-Catholicism in different segments of the population.

This simulation may be described as a data-rich, theory-poor simulation. There was a small set of interrelated propositions that constituted the basis of the simulation. These taken by themselves were reasonably well established, obvious, and not very powerful. They provided a routine, however, for processing a large body of good data. Recognition of this potential justified attempting a computer simulation.

There are, however, other instances where one should proceed with a computer simulation although one has very little data or none at all. One might do so where the parameter estimates (so numerous in the election simulation) are relatively few and can be provided by a variety of guesses, and where the interest of the simulation focuses on a highly complex, well-defined structure of propositions. An example of such a simulation is the Crisiscom simulation in which we feed messages into the computer that represents two decision makers. In processing these messages, the computer follows rules representing a number of psychological propositions about attention, retention, and information handling. The computer attempts to select for attention and recall those messages which a human decision maker would retain under the specified circumstances. We use absolutely no empirical measures of the decision makers. We set values for forgetting, salience, and other parameters arbitrarily. The interest of the simulation is in the process, not in the measures of particular real world parameter values. If psychologists had not provided us in recent years with a number of well-defined models of cognitive processes, the attempt to develop such a computer simulation would be absurd.

For a simulation to be computerizable, there must somewhere exist a complex structure of propositions and/or data values. But note that we have had to use the expression and/or. It is not true that both must exist. Thus, it is not necessarily true that a simulation is no more useful than its data.

Let me illustrate with an example that is indeed a total society simulation. In recent years I have worked on this simulation in two different forms. In an earlier form, known as the Media-Mix simulation, it represents the flow of messages through the mass media to the American population. In a more sophisticated form on which I am currently working, the Comcom simulation,[1] it represents the flow of messages through the mass media to the populations of the Soviet Union and China. In each of these simulations a population of a few thousand individuals is represented in the computer. These represent a sample of the population of the country. Each individual has certain social and demographic characteristics and also certain media habits. In the simulation a flow of messages is released to them through various media; the computer calculates the probability of a message having been re-

[1] This project is supported by the Advanced Research Projects Agency under contract No. 920F-9717 with the Center for International Studies, M.I.T., and monitored by the Air Force Office of Scientific Research under grant number AF(49)638-1237.

ceived by any given type of person after any given period of time.

This is a total society simulation. It is not a total simulation of a total society. It is a simulation of a single process, that of the flow of messages via the mass media, but for this selected aspect it examines, in a microcosm, the society as a whole. Any simulation of a total society is bound to be like that, i.e., it will be a representation of one or more aspects of the society. Just as either visible light or infra-red can provide a picture of an object, though in each case actually only reporting the object through one particular index of it, so a society can be indexed by any one of a number of pervasive aspects of it. Message flow is a good index because virtually every social process involves message flows. Exchange is another good index occurring in almost all social processes. So is power; so is role. That is why communication, economics, political science, and sociology are each effective ways of analyzing whole societies. Since these approaches are good ones for describing whole societies, they are good ones for simulating whole societies. In any case, the simulation we are here describing represents a society by its mass media message flow.

The three cases, the United States, the Soviet Union, and China, are of interest because they represent different points along the continuum from data richness to data poverty. For the United States we have Nielsen ratings, ABC circulation figures, media surveys of all sorts, exhaustively covering the facts about who reads and who listens to what. The Media-Mix simulation, like the Simulmatics election simulation, is essentially a large data processing operation. A resultant estimate of how many people have seen a particular advertisement how often, depends crucially upon audience figures for each of the media in which the ad appears.

In the Soviet case much data is available, but clearly nothing like the amount for the United States. There are good circulation figures for most important printed media. However, without sample surveys on pass-along readership, there are no good audience figures, nor are there anything like Nielsen ratings for the electronic media. There are, however, time budget studies describing people's time allocation to reading, radio listening, TV viewing, etc. In this instance one is combining good data with speculation to provide fair estimates.

For China our simulation is a form of fiction writing. Data is almost nonexistent. The Chinese published substantial data on newspaper circulation, production of radio sets and similar matters until 1958, as the curves were steadily rising. As soon as the curves stopped rising, they stopped publishing. Now that there has been some recovery from the catastrophe of the Great Leap Forward, a few series have again been reported. Nonetheless, one often has no figure even for such elementary items as the number of radios or the circulation of major newspapers or magazines. For the Chinese simulation to be worth undertaking, the body of propositions built into the simulation must be sufficiently powerful to produce results even with what is virtually guesswork data.

The first step in the simulation is to create a representative sample of the population. For China even that is difficult. Our estimates of the total population are poor. Our estimates of its division into rural and urban, literate and illiterate, male and female, are also poor. Our estimates of the interactions, e.g., of urban female literates, are almost nonexistent. From Frederick Mosteller we have derived a technique for estimating the numbers in each such combination cell, taking into account all interactions of which we have either knowledge or an estimate. So our first step is to draw from all our estimates of these interactions and of the marginal data an estimate of the structure of the Chinese population.

The next steps in the simulation are designed to produce estimates of probable media exposure by the persons in the population we have constructed. Typically, one arrives at an audience estimate by some kind of transformation of a circulation or set estimate. For example, we first work out estimates of the number of radios, the number of wired loudspeakers, total daily newspaper circulation, the total magazine circulation, total book publication, the circulations of specific major media publications, if we have any data, the number of minor media, the mean circulation of such minor media, the probable frequency distributions of circulations, etc. All of these circulation figures must then be multiplied by factors to provide audience estimates. Four hundred interviews with refugees in Hong Kong will help to provide a basis for estimating a set of factors by which circulation will have to be multiplied to arrive at estimated audience figures. Also, common sense and comparison with Soviet, American, and other figures will help provide a variety of numbers. The result of all of these manipulations is a set of single issue audience estimates for the various media, e.g., how many people in China hear Radio Peking in an evening.

These total audience estimates, however, are far less significant than their breakdown by population types. Once again we have some bases for differentiation, e.g., literacy figures for men and women, radio and wired loudspeaker figures for rural and urban areas, literacy figures for rural and urban areas. Once again we use the Mosteller technique to take account of all marginals about which we have information. The information, it should be noted, may be hard data or may be a hypothesis based upon knowledge of how communications media work around the world. Our simulation thus provides a set of estimates of audience by type of person for all of the main media.

Audience, however, is a static concept. It is the number of people exposed to a particular issue of a particular medium. To make our simulation dynamic we must take into account differences in audience habits. For example, a newspaper read by one million people each day might conceivably be read by one million people 365 times a year and never reach anyone else, or it might conceivably be read by 365 million different people, no one of them ever seeing more than one issue. The reality is, of course, somewhere in between. There is a distribution of readers by frequency, some seeing it daily, some seeing it once a year, and some with various intermediate frequencies. It is this distribution that is referred to by the concept of cumulation. No data exist from China about cumulation. However, there is data from other countries and we know that cumulation varies between media in various quite natural ways. Subscribers see a journal more frequently than non-subscribers. A professional journal is read by the same people over and over while a movie is seen by most people only once. Drawing on such foreign experience we estimate cumulation distributions for various media types.

Finally the simulation takes account of duplication. By duplication we mean the incidence of shared audience among different media. A classic study of duplication was Lazarsfeld's early volume on *Radio and the*

Printed Page, in which he found that, far from competing for news audiences, they tended to duplicate more than accidentally. Some people were news addicts, and would read newspapers as well as listen to news broadcasts. Others were not interested and therefore did neither. Again, we must concede that no Chinese data on duplication exists. Once again, we must apply factors to random duplication patterns to produce patterns predictable on the basis of foreign social research. The simulation takes all these mechanisms into account in accordance with the assigned parameter values and estimates exposures to the various media.

However, diffusion of a piece of information is not the same as diffusion of its medium. The final *pass* of the simulation therefore permits a scenario to be written about a *particular* piece of information. Suppose one is simulating the diffusion of knowledge of a crisis. One can postulate that only p percent of the audience for a given medium note a particular piece of information diffused by it. However, p need not be constant. In the early period of a crisis when the salience of the issues is low, p may be small. Later it may gradually rise. One can postulate that p varies with different groups in the population. Thus the simulation permits one to formulate a set of assumptions about the flow of news in a total society and to reach a specific conclusion with regard to those reached and how often. The conclusion will obviously be far more accurate for a situation like that of the United States—where almost all of the parameter estimates are based upon research—than it will be for China. Even so, for the latter, too, it will be a specific conclusion, a number that one can believe or disbelieve as one chooses. However, it will be a precise number, not some vague *ceteris paribus* statement that is unverifiable no matter what future empirical information we obtain.

To be more accurate we should concede that our simulation estimate is bound to be wrong. Like all measurements it has a standard error. Hypothetically, we may someday find out how big its standard error is. A statement of social science that is wrong but definite is better than the usual type whose main defense is a vagueness sufficient so that it cannot be *proved* wrong.

BIBLIOGRAPHY

American Behavioral Scientist. *Social Research with the Computer,* special issue, 1965, VIII, No. 9. (Contains descriptions of Comcom and Crisiscom simulations.)

Abelson, R. P. "Computer Simulation of Hot Cognition," in Tomkins, S. S., and Messick, S. *Computer Simulation of Personality,* New York: John Wiley, 1963.

————, and Bernstein, A. "A Computer Simulation Model of Community Referendum Controversies," *Public Opinion Quarterly,* 1963, XXVII, 93–122.

Archives Européennes de Sociologie. *Simulation in Sociology,* special issue, 1965, VI, No. 1.

Bauer, R. A., and Buzzell, R. D. "Mating Behavioral Science and Simulation," *Harvard Business Review,* 1964, XLII, 116–24.

Benson, O. "A Simple Diplomatic Game," in Rosenau, J. N. (ed.). *International Politics and Foreign Policy,* New York: The Free Press, 1961.

Berelson, Bernard, Lazarsfeld, Paul F., and McPhee, William N. *Voting,* Chicago: University of Chicago Press, 1954.

Beshers, J. M., and Reiter, S. "Social Status and Social Change," *Behavioral Science,* 1963, VIII, 1–14.

Borko, H. (ed.). *Computer Applications in the Behavioral*

Sciences, Englewood Cliffs, N.J.: Prentice Hall, 1962.

Browning, R. P. "Computer Programs as Theories of Political Processes," *Journal of Politics*, 1962, XXIV, 562–82.

Clarkson, G. P. S., and Simon, H. A. "Simulation of Group Behavior," *American Economic Review*, 1960, IV, 920–31.

Coleman, J. S. "Mathematical Models and Computer Simulation," in Faris, R. E. L. *Handbook of Modern Sociology*, Chicago: Rand McNally, 1964.

————. "The Use of Electronic Computers in the Study of Social Organizations," *Archives Européennes de Sociologie*, 1965, VI, 89–107.

Guetzkow, H. (ed.). *Simulation in Social Science*, Englewood Cliffs, N.J.: Prentice Hall, 1962.

Gullahorn, J., and Gullahorn, J. "A Computer Model of Elementary Social Behavior," in Feigenbaum, E. and Feldman, J., *Computers and Thought*, New York: McGraw Hill, 1965.

Hagerstrand, T. "A Monte Carlo Approach to Diffusion," in *Archives Européennes de Sociologie*, 1965, VI, 43–67.

Lazarsfeld, Paul F. *Radio and the Printed Page*, New York: Duell, Sloan and Pearce, 1940.

McPhee, W. N. *Formal Theories of Mass Behavior*, New York: The Free Press, 1963.

Pool, I. de S., Abelson, R. P., and Popkin, S. L. *Candidates, Issues, and Strategies: A Computer Simulation of the 1960 and 1964 Elections*, Cambridge, Mass.: M.I.T. Press, 1965.

————, and Kessler, A. "The Kaiser, the Tsar, and the Computer: Information Processing in a Crisis," *American Behavioral Scientist*, 1965, VIII, 31–39.

Popkin, S. L. "A Model of a Communication System," *American Behavioral Scientist*, 1965, VIII, 8–12.

Rainio, K. "Social Interaction as a Stochastic Learning Process," *Archives Européennes de Sociologie*, 1965, VI, 68–88.

————. *A Stochastic Theory of Social Contacts*, Copenhagen: Munksgaard, 1962.

Tomkins, S. S., and Messick, S. *Computer Simulation of Personality*, New York: John Wiley, 1963.

CONCEPTUAL ISSUES

EDWARD A. TIRYAKIAN

A MODEL OF SOCIETAL CHANGE
AND ITS LEAD INDICATORS

My intention here is to provide an ingress to the theory of change of total societies, which may be termed *macrodynamic sociology*. The materials will be divided into two major sections, reflecting what we consider to be two complementary problems in the scientific study of societal change. First, what is the nature or what are the major dimensions of societal change? Second, to what extent can societal change be predicted in advance?

The first problem will require a brief exposition of how a total society may be conceptualized, and the second will involve the notion (derived from Marxist thought) of "the revolutionary potential" of society, thus permitting us to suggest that a set of "lead indicators" may be specified with a high level of generality in predicting the occurrence of radical societal change.

However, it should be clearly understood that the model underlying the conceptualization set forth here is still in a preliminary state of development and formulation. A more refined presentation and adequate empirical verification is a matter of much additional work. Also, we shall not be able to trace all the intellectual sources and their specific contributions to this model, though it may be briefly indicated that we owe much to such thinkers as Durkheim, Weber, Sorokin, and Parsons, as well as to Marx and existential phenomenology. Finally, it should be remembered that this is not a general theory of all forms of social change (viz., short-term, random changes within institutional structures); it is a conceptualization intended as a heuristic device in exploring societal change in terms of the global society as a "total social phenomenon," to use Marcel Mauss's phrase.

A. CONCEPTUALIZING SOCIETAL CHANGE

A. 1. THE DEFINITION OF SOCIETAL CHANGE

By societal change will be understood the change in the organizational structure of a total society. Such a change is radical in the sense of being a total transformation of institutional structures, or approximating what Meusel calls "a recasting of the social order."[1] It is, therefore, fundamentally a *qualitative* change, a discontinuity or "leap" in the general normative pattern of the organization, which will be manifested in *all* major foci of institutional structure. What, therefore, distinguishes a revolution (see A.4) as a major type of societal change from other social upheavals is not the magnitude of physical violence, as is commonly argued, but its permeation of the social structure.

    A. 1. 1. Consider for example the social stratification system of the *ancien régime* and the modifications after the revolution. The abolition of hereditary privileges and deference based on ascriptive status is symbolized by the designations "citizen" and "comrade."

    A. 1. 2. Even the relation of social space to physical

[1] Alfred Meusel, "Revolution and Counter-Revolution," *Encyclopedia of the Social Sciences*, vol. 13 (New York: Macmillan, 1934 and 1942), p. 367.

space may be altered in the process of societal change. Thus in the case of the French Revolution, natural regions (provinces) were changed into more artificial "départements"; the metric system was adopted as part of the revolutionary overhaul, and even the basic temporal structure of the calendar was overthrown.

A. 2. SOCIETAL CHANGE AS A "RELIGIOUS" TRANSFORMATION

There are certain phenomena, inherent in true revolutions, that cannot be understood in terms of the criterion of rationality of action (i.e., viewing qualitative societal change as the result of political or economic grievances). To account for them, we have come to view societal change as essentially a "religious" transformation. By this is meant a very fundamental and dramatic form of religious experience, essentially one of death and rebirth.[2] A revolution affects the social order as the fire consumes the phoenix. It is in terms of an essentially "religious model" of the order underlying a total society (which will be discussed more extensively in A. 5 and B. 3. 3.) that we can comprehend phenomena such as a new basis of currency or changing the names of streets and even of the country itself. These are symbolic manifestations of what is involved in a revolution, even in one which is manifestly "secular" in its leadership.

A. 2. 1. In more "naturalistic" terms, the leap in organization involving the death and rebirth of the

[2] For an introduction to this exceedingly complicated and diffuse process, see Mircea Eliade, *The Sacred and the Profane* (New York: Harper Torchbooks, 1961), chapter 4.

societal system may be thought of as a type of *metamorphosis,* analogous to the transformation of the caterpillar into the butterfly. Moreover, although societal change involves a leap in structural organization, the new form of the social order will assume finite possibilities. The caterpillar has just one "degree of freedom" since its transformation is fixed by heredity.

A. 2. 2. *Inter alia,* I would suggest that, when studying radical societal change, it might be helpful to consider analogies in the physical and biological realms, e.g., the genetic *mutation,* and the leap of an outer electron from one energy level to another. In the case of the latter at least, despite an indeterminacy regarding the plane or orbital level on which the electron will "land," the possibilities are limited. Similarly, in societal transformations, it may be assumed the "degrees of freedom" are indeterminate but limited.

Nevertheless, analogies are not identities. In terms of our model, a crucial element is our perspective of societal change as intense social "purification" and "renewal". This psychological-symbolic dimension does not exist in physical or biological systems manifesting discontinuities, and is thus beyond analogy. However, there is one phenomenon that may be homologous to qualitative societal transformations: the experience, at the level of personality structure, of sudden transformations in the nature of "conversion" experiences. Unfortunately, our understanding of this phenomenon is too tenuous to be conclusive.

A. 3. THE RELATION OF SOCIAL TO SOCIETAL CHANGE

We take social change to be essentially a continuous rather than a discontinuous process. It is a quantitative elaboration of structural differentiation.[3] *Social* change is characterized by quantitative increments within a certain pattern of organization, within a certain institutional structure. *Societal* change, as a discontinuous process of structural innovation, is nevertheless linked with social change. We are concerned here with the complex notion of the dialectical process by which the quantitative gives rise to the qualitative and vice versa.

To use a familiar analogy, as the temperature of water is increased from $32°$ F. to $212°$ F. by continuous increments, there is no qualitative change in the state of H_2O. However, when the boiling point is reached, there is a sudden qualitative change that is contingent on all previous quantitative ones.

Thus, a presupposition of our model is that societal and social change are interdependent but analytically distinct, and, further, that societal change is not "random" or even "irrational." Instead, it is a dramatic response to pressures built up from within the society in question. Beyond a hypothesized "threshold" of structural tolerance for system-induced strains, there will be a breakdown in the system of organization. This structural breakdown is often attended by a reconstruction of the social order at a new level of organization, which always implies commitment to a new set of societal values and goals (and therefore the negation of the previous set of societal norms).

[3] Cf. Talcott Parsons, "Some Considerations on the Theory of Social Change," *Rural Sociology*, 26 (September 1961), p. 220.

A. 4. REVOLUTIONS AND SOCIETAL CHANGE

Revolutions rather than less comprehensive upheavals are the empirical referents of our model. That is, societal change is a revolutionary transformation of the structure of the social order, not evolutionary. We diverge from previous sociological literature, however, in our refusal to consider large-scale physical violence to be the hallmark of revolutions. The structural conditions that in one instance may favor violent political revolution may elsewhere suggest quite different solutions. Essentially, the "leap" in structural organization involved in societal change may, in public life, become externalized in either the political *or* the economic sphere. The rationale for this will be discussed in section A. 5. We may note here that, according to preliminary and still tentative research, the prevalent structural conditions of mid-eighteenth-century France were also those of England. Instead of political revolution, England experienced a nonviolent transformation of its societal ethos (in large part due, perhaps, to the impetus of Methodism). Societal change seems to have been effected through socioeconomic and sociocultural activities, e.g., philanthropy, entrepreneurial pursuits, missionary and educational movements. This example indicates that the short-term radical transformation of the system of production and distribution of goods and facilities, including its normative framework (its *Wirtschaftsethik*) amounts to a revolution as fundamental as that created by a radical change in the distribution of political power.

It may be well to indicate the delimitations of our perspective on revolutions.

A. 4. 1. We do not pay attention to lesser (microsocial) political upheavals such as rebellions, insurrections, and other instances of "internal war," including in this category "palace revolutions" of pre-Castro Latin America or the pre-Nasser Middle East. Traditional palace revolutions, for example, serve only to illustrate that "the more things change the more they remain the same." In this context, turnover among the régime's incumbents only serves to validate the structure of the social order.

A. 4. 2. We shall waive the question of the viability of revolutions as direct exports, either economically or politically; nor are we particularly interested at this stage of theoretical formulation with the teleological or purposeful aspects of revolutions. Of course, revolutions may have as a *sufficient* cause a small, highly organized group of individuals consciously seeking via rational actions to overthrow the political or economic state of affairs ("revolutionaries" or "conspirators" in the political context, "entrepreneurs" in the economic context). However, it is here contended that a sustained transformation requires antecedent *necessary* conditions (structural prerequisites, in Levy's sense[4]) that may well have no direct or manifest relation to the objectives of the revolutionaries. In fact, these antecedents may have developed over a long period of time at various "depth" levels of the social structure. They may not even be publicly recognized, although there may be some awareness of a general "malaise" or "unrest."

If a revolution is considered as a tendency to-

---

[4] Marion Levy, Jr., *The Structure of Society* (Princeton: Princeton University Press, 1952), pp. 71–76.

ward total transformation of societal structure (*id est*, as approximating a 180° rotation of the social order), its mass appeal may well be different in character from its appeal to those wishing explicitly a radical political (or alternatively economic) change. A revolution, to be successful, requires the contingent support of the people; but mass support, by its very nature, may be a response to a different (although, perhaps, overlapping) set of conditions from those that motivate a revolutionary "intelligentsia," or "articulation leaders."[5] While it is to the advantage of such élites to be identified with the masses, there may be important differentials in the fundamental aims of revolutionary commitment. This contention, of course, requires documentation that is beyond our present scope.

A. 4. 3. Another prime phenomenon in considering the change of a total society is the notion of *crisis*, i.e., the period during which societal change becomes manifest, when the imminence of the structural transformation becomes reliably apparent to most observers, but before the outcome of the impending leap is discernible. This notion of crisis is derived from pathology, where crisis is identified as that moment in the course of a serious disease when the resolution is uncertain.

By extension, a revolution is a societal *catharsis*[6]

[5] The latter designation is used by David Willer and George K. Zollschan, "Prolegomenon to a Theory of Revolutions," in George K. Zollschan and Walter Hirsch, eds., *Explorations in Social Change* (Boston: Houghton Mifflin, 1964), p. 138.

[6] "It is by means of national calamities that a national corruption must cure itself," (*Lettre de Bolingbroke*, cited in F. Le Play, *Les Ouvriers Européens*, 2nd ed., volume 1, *La Méthode d'Observation* (Tours: Alfred Mame et Fils, 1879), p. 1.

—essentially, a drastic purification of a social structure in fundamental disorder, expressing the loss of solidarity between rulers and ruled, and the emergence in the public institutional sphere of normally suppressed societal phenomena (one form of which is discussed in B. 3. 2.). Thus a revolution is both an end state, the culmination of a process of structural dissolution, and simultaneously it is also a radical instance of what Howard Becker called a "normative reaction to normlessness."[7]

The crisis represents the crucial transition point at which the developing revolution can establish itself, basically, according to one of two major institutional "options": a constructive (non-violent) *socioeconomic* "leap"[8] or a destructive (violent) sociopolitical *transformation*. In concrete instances this is not an either/or case, but in the event, one or the other will predominate.[9] It is in part the indeterminacy of the outcome that underlies our idea of the degree of freedom inherent in total societies and societal change.

A. 4. 4. It should be obvious that, depending on the strategy and value-orientation of those concerned (e.g., revolutionaries, counter-revolutionaries, and

[7] Howard Becker, "Normative Reactions to Normlessness," *American Sociological Review*, 25 (December 1960), pp. 803–10.

[8] I have in mind here the theory of economic "take-off" propounded by W. W. Rostow, *The Stages of Economic Growth* (Cambridge University Press, 1960).

[9] It may be suggested that a fundamental dilemma of total societies in the modern setting is whether to opt for rapid economic development or rapid political development, the former being a centrifugal force, the latter a centripetal one. We would argue that they cannot be maximized simultaneously; the price of economic development is the erosion of social cohesion.

status quo upholders), it would be highly desirable to be able to pinpoint the crisis "moment." It is at such times that a concerted effort on the part of a small but highly organized group can act as a lever. The crisis situation is sufficiently ambiguous at a general societal level for those with an adequate "definition of the situation" to utilize the previously generated revolutionary momentum to crucial advantage. Of course, if the societal transformation runs its course, the revolution that develops along political lines is also likely to manifest a secondary crisis period of ambiguity and societal destructuration. This period has frequently captured the imagination of writers on revolutions, but it might be more intellectually interesting to treat it as a Shakespearian fifth act *dénouement*, while redirecting attention to the more significant third act crisis.

Thus, the outcome of the Russian societal crisis that reached its culmination in 1917 could have been either a political or an economic revolution. The crisis, however, may well have occurred not in 1917 but at least a decade before, with the events of 1904–5 quite likely providing the key turning point.

A. 5. A CONCEPTUALIZATION OF THE SOCIETAL SYSTEM

As will be apparent, we are heavily indebted to Talcott Parsons for his formulation of a general theory of action. From his analysis of the major structures of social systems we derive the following structural differentiation of a total society:

	A		G	
	economy		polity	

PROFANE

SACRED

	L		I	
	recreation		kinship	
	religion		law	
	education			

We assume that the basic A-G-I-L (*A*daptive, *G*oal Attainment, *I*ntegrative, *L*atency—pattern maintenance, tension management) categorization developed by Parsons, and its rationale, are familiar to readers of this paper [A capsule explanation is found in the paper by Klausner, pp. 9–12. Ed.]: as part of this systems analysis a total society is heuristically considered as differentiated into four major structures, each focusing upon basic problems for social existence (integration of members, adaptation to environmental exigencies, purposeful ends, tension-management, etc.).[10]

A. 5. 1. Although Parsons has been greatly interested in the interchanges between structures, it is the A and G (notably the economy and the polity) that have received most of his attention. These we consider the key aspects of "public life" (the German term *Öffentlichkeit* is apposite). They also correspond to what Durkheim considered the loci of

[10] See, for example, Talcott Parsons, *The Social System* (New York: Free Press, 1951); Parsons and Shils, ed., *Toward a General Theory of Action* (Cambridge: Harvard University Press, 1951); Parsons, *et. al.*, eds., *Theories of Society* (New York: Free Press, 1961).

"profane" activities in contradistinction to the "sacred."

On the other hand, we have been more preoccupied with the L and I sectors, in particular with the L-cell, which Parsons by a fortunate coincidence terms the "latency" structure. We shall use the term "latency" to suggest that in this sector the fundamental but predominantly covert processes of social transformation originate and are disseminated.[11] This sector is the one oriented to the *grounds of meaning* of the total society, including the basic value premises that articulate the society's perception of reality, and that underlie the organization of major social institutions. It is in the L-structure, then, that the fundamental patterns, or structures, of social order are to be located.

A. 5. 2. Accordingly, the L-cell may be differentiated into four major subparts:

L_A	L_G
"pure" science art (painting, sculpture, etc.)	institutional religion (Church, denomination) formal education
L_L	L_I
non-institutional religion	amusements/recreation (theater, spectacles, etc.)

[11] This parallels Georges Gurvitch's analysis of "hidden" dimensions of societal structure. See Georges Gurvitch, ed., *Traité de Sociologie* (Paris: Presses Universitaires de France, 1958), Part II, chapter 1 ("Sociologie en Profondeur"), and also p. 238.

Albeit the L_G and L_I subsystems are integrated into the larger society to a relatively major extent, the L_A and L_I also have *non-institutional* aspects—and even *anti-institutional* possibilities—which are not for "public consumption." Thus, even "pure" scientific research has very often been cloaked in secrecy, from its début in alchemy to the present (e.g., nuclear research). The sector of "recreation" (or "tension-release") contains in turn activities often so ambiguous that they may act not so much to "stabilize" the system and its ground of meaning but also to "undermine" it. Dialectically speaking, recreation also involves destruction; what is manifestly "funny" can have extremely serious consequences, a sociological fact that underlies the practice of censorship of the arts; left to their own devices, various forms of entertainment can "contaminate" and nihilate what is institutionally "decorous."

The Paris crowds, who, in the 1770s and 1780s, saw plays lampooning George III and extolling the American rebels, were treated to more than anti-British propaganda. It was evident that the theme of American political emancipation constituted an indirect attack on the French monarchy as well. Similarly, many Negro "spirituals" of the slavery period were not merely expressions of resignation, but also a means of idealized liberation from actual conditions. Currently, the so-called "folk singers" utilize a manifest recreational activity and setting to advocate political radicalism.

A. 5. 3. The major focus of the model under consideration is in this context the L_L cell wherein we locate non-institutional religious phenomena, i.e., those not treated as part of the conventional, respectable, or "mainstream" way of life—those outside the "Establishment." Nevertheless, such phenomena embody the most fundamental ("elementary" in Durkheim's sense) forms of collective sentiments. Moreover, because they are not institutionalized (or routinized) they manifest the greatest psychological intensity. It is here that "charisma" or religious enthusiasm (as noted by Weber) manifests itself, the point at which sacred and profane commingle.

In our model of total societies, we assume that the basic foundation of the social order is essentially a moral (religious-normative) one. That is, the general "way of life" or "world-view" of a society is an all-encompassing structure of structures (*societal* structure) that by virtue of its fundamentality is and must be considered "sacred." Therefore, societal change involves a fundamental redefinition of the situation, a negation of the moral validity of the existent social order and a new basic religious/sacred reorientation that simultaneously is a desacralization of the *status quo*. The non-institutional religious sphere provides the grounds for *mass* (not élite) rejection of the constitutive structure of society.[12]

The religious sphere has a double societal function: to provide the major basis of legitimation for a social order, and to be the major source of inspiration for illegitimizing it. *Religion is a major vehicle for both the status quo and societal*

[12] Moreover, it is very possible that some of the inspiration for élite-intellectual rejection of the societal order may itself spring from unrecognized religious sources rather than from rational-pragmatic considerations. Such sources need not be identical to those operative in the masses.

change. The L_L sector is strategically located as a lever for societal change; religious phenomena, particularly non-institutional ones (cults, sects, messianic and chiliastic movements, quasi-religious secret societies, etc.) are in the furthest recesses of privacy, in part because they appear so "irrational" to outsiders. Hence they are a refuge from public scrutiny and forms of social control. Whereas other sectors and institutions may be "corrupted" through processes of compromise inevitable in the process of institutionalization,[13] the non-institutional religious sphere, by its very nature morally homogeneous, remains intensely pure—a potential source of social purification.

A. 5. 4. To recapitulate, it is in the covert, non-institutional sphere of society that new basic meanings, innovations or radical renovations of cultural definitions of the situation are generated as responses to societal strains. The sector termed the L_L subfield functions (not by rational design, of course) to keep total societies "open" systems. (In religious imagery, it does so by allowing the Spirit or charisma to renovate institutions and re-establish social cohesion.) It is precisely such patterns of sociocultural meaning, having binding implications for various other institutional sectors, that constitute real societal change. Because the irruption of charisma (or enthusiasm as studied by Knox[14]) is as sudden and abrupt in its manifesta-

[13] See Thomas O'Dea, "Sociological Dilemmas: Five Paradoxes of Institutionalization," in Edward A. Tiryakian, ed., *Sociological Theory, Values, and Sociocultural Change: Essays in Honor of Pitirim A. Sorokin* (New York: Free Press, 1963), pp. 71–89.

[14] Ronald A. Knox, *Enthusiasm* (New York: Oxford University Press, 1950; Galaxy Books, 1961).

tions as it is infrequent, we attribute to societal change characteristics of discontinuity.

Of course, it is undeniable that revolutions (political or economic) have elements of conscious, rational planning. Obviously, societal overthrow must entail some degree of rational planning. It is even quite likely that a multiplicity of groups of varying degrees of organization may at varying degrees of rationality and consciousness orient their action to the destruction of the societal order. Yet that which appeals to the intellectual élite and its ancillary supporters will not necessarily make sense to the rank-and-file (as Peter the Great—and administrators of a multitude of foreign aid programs—discovered). Our model supposes that the mass support necessary for a revolution is a spiritual-emotional response to broad underlying conditions that seldom figure in revolutionary ideology.

B. PREDICTING SOCIETAL CHANGE

B. 1. METHODOLOGICAL PROBLEMS

Are revolutions or other violent upheavals predictable? If we formulate societal change as one involving a qualitative "leap" in the basic societal ground of meaning that transforms institutional structure within a short period of time, how are sociological predictions of such discontinuities possible?

B. 1. 1. Part of the problem involves the question of isolating the necessary sociological components of a revolution. A social revolution represents the global society in upheaval, but research done on revolutions suffers, on the one hand, from an inadequate conceptualization of the essential qualitative factors involved, and on the other hand from the fact that it is only quite recently that serious quantitative research has been undertaken on differentials in revolutionary participation, etc.[15]

Hitherto, revolutions have been seen as political manifestations and no general conceptualization has been formulated that would encompass the structure and dynamics of both economic and political revolutions. Yet, we hold these to be complementary and integral parts of a general theory of societal change.

(Since I would prefer to be suggestive rather than conclusive, I might venture that a theory of societal change may also consider revolutions and world wars as complementary. This is analogous to the view in clinical psychology that homicide and suicide are interrelated phenomena of aggression.)

Furthermore, since it is the more vulgar, physical aspects of violence that have captured the imagination, revolutions have been treated as extreme secular political agitation, whereas we tend to place stress on their very deep and explosive religious symbols of purification, death and rebirth (or redemption), with frequently obscure apocalyptic and chiliastic inspiration.

In addition, the question of predicting radical transformations in the social system has received attention mainly from the Marxist perspective,

[15] Charles Tilly and James Rule, *Measuring Political Upheaval* (Princeton: Princeton University, Center of International Studies, 1965).

which focuses upon the "objective" characteristics of a pre-revolutionary setting. When the objective (socioeconomic) state of the "proletariat" is taken as sufficiently pauperized relative to that of the ruling bourgeoisie, there the *revolutionary potential* (see B. 2) is considered to be of sufficient magnitude for the propitious launching of a revolution.

The trouble with this approach is that socioeconomic or "objective" conditions are insufficient to determine the stability or instability of any given society, and that more "subjective" factors also play a crucial part. These include the extent of trust between official rulers and the population and the degree of commitment of rulers to the social order they are meant to represent, i.e., the amount of self-confidence of incumbent officials with respect to their legitimacy.

To see weakness in the "pure" Marxist materialistic model, we need only consider how badly Marx misjudged the revolutionary situation of post-1848 Europe (where objective conditions would have led one to predict a revolution in England and other industrial societies). Lenin and Trotsky implicitly recognized this weakness by creating the party as the self-fulfilling prophet, since, left to its own devices, the proletariat could not—or would not?—bring about the revolution dictated by objective conditions. However, if Marx went wrong it may not have been because of technological changes, as is commonly argued, so much as the result of changes in the effective ruling classes of Western Europe and in their normative behavior. It may have been precisely the sobriety, asceticism, religiosity, and future-orientation of the new bourgeois entrepreneurial

class that gave the Victorian Age the *élan* and
the ethos to stifle a political revolution. Furthermore, since I do not consider economic grievances
to be determining causes of revolutions, I would
argue that the likelihood of revolution has little
to do with either industrial development or un-
derdevelopment. Only ostriches would think that
the standard of living of blue-collar workers in
the Western nations, including the United States,
provides immunity from revolutions—with or
without a Communist Party.

B. 1. 2. I submit that the prediction of societal
change cannot be based on economic conditions.
Such a prediction, however fraught with problems, can be conceptualized as a meaningful possibility. It is analogous to predicting critical turns
in the primary movement of the stock market
(from bullish to bearish and vice versa). Pursuing this analogy, is it possible to find in the social
structure phenomena or aspects of the total society that give sufficient warning of an impending
"leap" of structural organization, as significant as
the price of IBM is as a lead indicator of short-
term market behavior, or the Index of Commodity
Prices as a long-term lead indicator? A composite
of such societal indicators may appropriately be
called the *index of revolutionary potential* (R_p)
of society, and if capable of quantification, we
could construct a reliable index of the revolutionary potential ($I R_p$).

B. 2. CONCEPTUALIZING THE INDEX OF REVOLUTIONARY POTENTIAL

A rigorous sociological treatment of the revolutionary potential of society is lacking in the literature,

though Feldman has recently made a step in this direction.[16]

We shall conceptualize the R_p as a propensity for social disorder, or alternatively, as a gauge or a barometer of social instability. It follows that the complement of the R_p is a measure of social stability.[17] Any given total society may be located, at least theoretically, on the following "barometer":

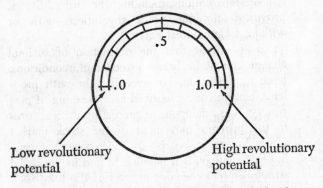

Low revolutionary potential

High revolutionary potential

B. 2. 1. We have arbitrarily designated the limits as zero and one, with continuous intervals in between. The former would be a state customarily called a "utopia," one with a nonexistent R_p. This implies that the social structure in which R_p

16 Arnold S. Feldman, "Violence and Volatility: The Likelihood of Revolution," in Harry Eckstein, ed., *Internal War* (New York: Free Press, 1964), pp. 111–29.

17 And therefore not of the propensity for a counter-revolution; the counter-revolutionary potential is of the same magnitude as the R_p, at least in our conceptualization. Stated differently, from a theoretical consideration the chances of a counter-revolution occurring are of the same magnitude as those of a revolution. An excellent strategy of revolutionaries is to place counter-revolutionaries in the position of supporting (rather than attacking) the social order precisely at that time when the ship of state is about to tilt.

equals zero is so viable, in terms of both external and internal exigencies, that there is such a perfect balance of forces making for social order (which does not exclude the possibility of conflict), that no element or group of the population is committed to or contemplating a new basic patterning of social organization; nor are there structural strains that would be conducive to a radical transformation.

Objectively, there is no discrepancy between the social norms underlying social institutions and the actual empirical practices or role relationships embodying these norms. Finally, in such a state all the members comprise, or think they comprise, a homogeneous moral community. Such a state is clearly a limiting condition.

B. 2. 2. At the other extreme, a measure of one indicates that the R_p is passing into the revolutionary actual; at this point there occurs a societal upheaval or transformation observable in all institutions. The "old order" is eliminated. Barometric readings of one can only be infrequent, perhaps occurring for just brief spans of time. They represent moments of anarchy or total societal destructuration, or suspension of institutionalized modes of procedure (political, economic, cultural); it is here that we find a radical denial of the legitimacy of previous institutions. In brief, it represents the explosion of the moral community that constituted the society.[18]

[18] At the micro-social level, disasters or catastrophes present in their "emergency phase" ambiguous situations which are of the same sort as revolutionary periods at the macro-social level. For a conceptualization of disasters, see my paper, "Aftermath of a Thermonuclear Attack on the United States: Some Socio-

Although, at the point one, the social turbulence should be most manifest (in the case of political revolution), this does not imply that all the members of society are committed ideologically to the overthrow of the social order, i.e., to the radical redefinition of the fundamental patterns of meaning (any more than at the point zero, or close to it, all are *committed* to the normative way of life and its embodiments). It is my opinion that those consciously seeking to promote a revolution (economic as well as political), i.e., with a definite radical conception of the social order they rationally seek to create, can only be a small minority of the adult population (perhaps less than 20 per cent in any case and probably less than 5 per cent in most cases). But the same number of "revolutionaries" will find that their chances of success rise as the R_p rises—assuming that the latter is not directly owing to the actions of the former.

The R_p may also be thought of as a probabilistic statement with respect to the likelihood of revolution. Thus a reading of .5 would be taken to indicate that the chances of revolution are 50–50. The higher the probability, the greater the objective manifestations of the R_p, and the more difficult it will be for existing agencies of social control to prevent its outbreak and restore the social equilibrium. Above a level of, say, .85, one may anticipate that the course of events will precipitate either a revolution, a counter-revolution, or perhaps an equally radical alternative, the structural disintegration and fragmentation of the

logical Considerations," *Social Problems,* 6 (Spring 1959), pp. 291–303.

social system (e.g., the collapse of the Roman Empire).

B. 2. 3. Certainly, we are by no means ready to suggest how to operationalize such an R_p scale or barometer. However, a crude initial approach may be got by asking a panel competent in comparative analysis to assign ratings to several countries: perhaps England, the United States, Russia, Cuba, Egypt, Switzerland, Israel, South Africa, Guinea and Mexico. What sort of gradations would be obtained from a panel of judges[19] and what factors would be adduced in evaluating the R_p? What sort of questions would be necessary to enable the panel to give a meaningful assignment?

B. 2. 4. It might be well to keep in mind that all "modern" societies (which in part implies ideological commitment to change) may have a rather high endemic R_p, which is necessary if the capacity to maintain modernization is to be retained. By way of analogy, humans require a high blood temperature, and a fall below, say, 96° F. would be as incapacitating as a rise above 99° F. A certain R_p, then, is reflective of a certain state of tension in the society which has both functional and dysfunctional aspects.

B. 3. LEAD INDICATORS

Our conceptualization of societal change and the R_p has led us to consider what "advance warning signals" there may be of the revolutionary outbreak. Such indicators should have an optimal lead time, in the sense

---

[19] For heuristic purposes, at least, I would suggest that the United States has a very high R_p, Israel a very low one, with the other countries occupying intermediate positions.

that if they are too close to the revolution, e.g., with an R_p reading of .96 they would be banal reflections of critical conditions, yet if too far away in time from the revolution they would also lose their purpose, e.g., predicting in the year 1392 that France was going to have a major social revolution would mean very little. Three indicators would seem to be significantly related to the outbreak of a revolution; in terms of preliminary and still highly tentative research, their lead time is about 10–30 years. These indicators are:

B. 3. 1. *Significant increases in rates of urbanization.* This factor is adduced in the light of theoretical propositions to be found in Durkheim and Simmel concerning the significance of numbers for social organization. The argument, essentially, is that there are empirical limits to types of social organization and social structures; beyond demographic and ecological limits, the efficiency of social institutions and social structure will be impaired.

Furthermore, the rapid concentration of people in a confined space also intensifies the likelihood of increased irritability and social pathology.[20] Paradoxically, the diffusion of irritability may facilitate revolutionary violence, since violence of an extreme sort may be thought of as a means of tension-reduction (analogous to electric shock therapy). In any case, attention should be given to the fact that "great social upheavals lessen the frequency of delinquency and mental disorders."[21] It is plausible that these are conse-

[20] John B. Calhoun, "Population Density and Social Pathology," *Scientific American,* vol. 206 (February 1962), pp. 139–48.

[21] Frantz Fanon, *The Wretched of the Earth* (New York: Grove Press, 1965), p. 248.

quences of a rapid increase in population density. It is necessary to specify intervening variables, but this would take us too far afield.

Other considerations justify the use of this lead indicator, but it is enough to stress that this is a testable proposition if we examine historical revolutions, and that the sheer magnitude of the urban population is of less interest than changes in the *rates* of urbanization.

B. 3. 2. *Significant increases in the distribution and public acceptance of sexual promiscuities.* Social organization may be considered in terms of a continuum of *hedonism-asceticism.* When public life is highly ascetic, we postulate a low R_p because of a tight social integration. Social organization involves, among other things, the subordination of sexual and other forms of hedonistic gratification (or in Parsonian terminology, "consummatory activities" which are by nature self-oriented) to socially constructive, goal-oriented "instrumental" activities. A sudden significant increase in hedonistic behavior matched with a legitimation and/ or a public acceptance of this implies a severe state of *anomie;* the flaunting of promiscuity in public life, what we may call *sexual anomie,* implies a loss of the normative cohesion of the society in question. It implies a desacralization of the fundamental patterns of meaning. Of course, sexual promiscuity or "tabula rasa" practices are to be found in all societies, but the crucial point is that when the ruling class and the performing arts (the L_I sector in the Parsonian model) can with impunity depict social reality in terms of sexual promiscuity and symbols of degradation, this is indicative of deep, non-institutional disturbances in the social structure.[22]

That revolution brings about a purification in public morality is observable no matter which example one considers: the French Revolution, the English Industrial Revolution, the Soviet, the Chinese Communist, or the Cuban. Thus, the purifying, puritanical aspects of revolutionaries or those who assume power in the wake of revolution (e.g., Cromwell, Robespierre, Lenin) may be of crucial appeal to a broad spectrum of the population disillusioned with the failure of the ruling class or governing institutions to control sexual morality. England escaped the fate of France in the 18th century primarily because English Methodism and the nonconformist churches provided at a strategic time a new ruling, entrepreneurial class characterized by a high degree of asceticism.

B. 3. 3. *Significant increases in the outbreak of non-institutional religious phenomena.* Non-institutional religious phenomena include outbreaks of glossolalia, messianic and chiliastic movements, the appearance of new cults and sects, and other groups not publicly "respectable."

With regard to African Separatist and Independent Church movements, it has been noted that religious messianism and separatism was an important and crucial forerunner of African political nationalism and independence. It provided the basis for militant rejection of the colonial social order, i.e., religious radicalism was instru-

---

[22] This has been well noted by Pitirim A. Sorokin in his study (still the most comprehensive sociological treatment of revolutions), *The Sociology of Revolution* (Philadelphia: J. B. Lippincott, 1925), Chapter 6.

mental in destroying belief in the legitimacy of
colonialism. Structurally, this functioned much
the way the Protestant Reformation did in six-
teenth- and seventeenth-century Europe, when it
destroyed belief in the "natural" authority of
Rome and thus fostered political upheaval.

Subsequent investigations in the etiology of
other revolutions have indicated that a religious
"revival" or effervescence is an antecedent condition, providing a lead time of about 25–35 years.

Theoretical justification for this indicator as a
valid correlation may be stated as follows: If we
accept the notion that social revolutions essentially
involve a fundamental reordering of the social
structure, and if we accept the supposition that
the social order is essentially viewed as a moral
phenomenon by the members of the collectivity,
then there must be a new source of morality involved in societal change, one that both desacral-
izes the present system and paves the way for the
acceptance of a new order. (This is the death and
rebirth aspect of social revolutions.) Since established religion represents a compromise with
the on-going secular institutions, the only other
possible host of revolutionary thought, however
unwittingly, is the non-institutional religious sector. (It may be recalled that at first the new Chris-
tian sect(s) was considered subversive by existing
religious and political authorities.)

CONCLUSION

The methodological pitfalls involved in the formulation of a model of societal change are numerous; I

may well have stumbled into some of them here. Nevertheless, it is hoped that the outlines of the model presented above will have heuristic value in redirecting attention to problems and dimensions inherent in the conceptualization of societal change.

To recapitulate, I view societal change as a macrosocial phenomenon that can be analytically differentiated from microsocial phenomena of social change. Moreover, societal change is essentially a profound transformation in the normative structure of a society —a rotation of the societal axis that takes a long time to be fully institutionalized—but one whose inauguration is sharply and dramatically manifested as a "leap" in societal organization. I have suggested that the revolutionary potential of a total society may be manifested in lead indicators to be found in areas of the social structure removed from the actual foci of the revolutionary outbreak (economic or political), particularly in the non-institutional sphere, i.e., the "social underground" or "grass roots" of society.

REFERENCES

Arendt, Hannah. *On Revolution* (New York: The Viking Press, 1963).

Davis, James C. "Toward a Theory of Revolution," *American Sociological Review*, 27 (February 1962), pp. 5–19.

Edward, Lyford P. *The Natural History of Revolution* (Chicago: The University of Chicago Press, 1927).

Ellwood, Charles A. "A Psychological Study of Revolutions," *American Journal of Sociology*, 11 (July 1905), pp. 49–59.

Janne, Henri. "Un modèle théorique du phénomène révolutionnaire?" *Annales: Economies, Sociétés, Civilisations*, 15e année, no 6. 1960, pp. 1138–54.

Martin, Everett Dean. *Farewell to Revolution* (London: Routledge and Sons, Ltd., 1936).

Meusel, Alfred. "Revolution and Counter-Revolution," *Encyclopedia of the Social Sciences,* vol. 13 (New York: Macmillan, 1934 and 1942), pp. 367–76.

Smelser, Neil J. *Theory of Collective Behavior* (New York: The Free Press, 1963), esp. chapter 10.

Sorokin, Pitirim A. *The Sociology of Revolution* (Philadelphia: J. B. Lippincott, 1925).

———. *Man and Society in Calamity* (New York: E. P. Dutton, 1942).

Zollschan, George, and Hirsch, Walter, eds. *Explorations in Social Change* (Boston: Houghton Mifflin, 1964).

KENNETH E. BOULDING

THE LEARNING PROCESS IN THE DYNAMICS OF TOTAL SOCIETIES

A dynamic process is a succession of states, S_1, S_2 . . . S_n, of a system at successive points in time. Dynamic systems are present if there are patterns in the succession of states. The simplest of these patterns is the difference equation, or the differential equation, but of course many other patterns are possible. We may consider the dynamic process as a four-dimensional continuum in space and time, and if there are dynamic systems, this continuum will exhibit patterns which have some property of repetition. We can think of it almost as a four-dimensional wallpaper. The present moment is a boundary in this four-dimensional continuum, from which we look backward into an image of the past, derived essentially from information contained in deposits which the past has made—fossils, writings, buildings, artifacts, and memories. Because we are able to build up an image of the past which has some sort of order and pattern to it, we are able to project this pattern to some extent into the future. The further we go from the present, of course, either into the past or the future, the less clear the patterns become. In the case of the past this is because the channels of information become fewer the further back we go. In the case of the future it is because of the presence of elements in the system which are random from the point of view of the observer, that is, which cannot be fitted into any known pattern. The proportion of the total pattern involving these random elements increases as we move into the future, and the possibility of predicting becomes less; that is, the subjective probability which we might attach to any particular image of the future becomes less as the future becomes more remote and as we look further and further into it.

Our ability to develop and perceive patterns in the past depends on two things, the information channels which extend back into the past and our ability to develop abstractions, that is, models, with which to filter, arrange, and interpret the information received from the past. Such information is carried by those objects or structures that exhibit some kind of stability through time, e.g., rocks, fossils, buildings, monuments, inscriptions, books, records, and memories. If we know the law of dynamic change of a structure, then we can project its present condition into the past and know what it was like at various dates in the past. Thus an archaeologist can take a ruin and reconstruct it as the building it must once have been; he can even deduce many things about the nature of the culture that produced it, since there are certain regularities in the transformation of buildings into ruins. Similarly, ancient texts can be reconstructed because there are certain consistencies of textual corruption through copying. In the case of Carbon 14 dating, we use a constant process of radioactive decay to project an existing structure back into the past, thus establishing the date when atmospheric carbon was captured by the object in question. In the case of rocks and fossils, there may be no decay at all, and we can project their existing structure for hundreds of millions of years into the past.

This, however, is only a special case of the general principle of projection by means of known patterns of change. One of the problems in constructing an image of the past is that the patterns of change are only imperfectly known, and the further back we attempt to project anything, the more subject to uncertainty our reconstructions will be. Another great problem we face is that the information provided by the past is inevitably a strongly biased sample; biased, for instance, in favor of durability of structure, of written communications rather than the oral ones that leave no permanent record except in the memory trace. We know very little, for example, about the origins of spoken language, because they have left no clues in bones or artifacts. In the post-telephonic present, the lot of the historian has been made harder by the fact that there has been a shift from written to spoken communications in the process of decision making. Hence the record of many important steps in these processes is irretrievably lost, even though a final decision is usually embodied in permanent written form.

The development of abstract models of social systems performs a number of essential functions. It is necessary in the first place because even though the information obtained from the past may be limited, it is still so large in volume that unless there is some method of organization and selection it will produce noise rather than knowledge. As I have suggested many times elsewhere, knowledge is achieved by the orderly loss of information, not by piling bit on bit. Another essential function of the abstract model is that it enables us to detect deficiencies in the information flow itself, and to deduce what we lack from what we have. A model is something like a jigsaw puzzle: even when many of the pieces are missing we can still be aware of the fact and can have some idea of the nature of the information they would contain. However,

e nature of the bias in the sample of information
om the past remains a very difficult problem, one for
hich we may never find a complete solution.

Models of social processes may be misleading as well
helpful. If the models themselves are inadequate,
ey will lead the investigator to eliminate information
hich may be highly relevant to his problem. Con-
rsely, they may include irrelevant information. This
the danger of all simple interpretations of history.
he conventional historian, for instance, who concen-
ates on the dynasties and the wars that feature so
ominently in the written record, is apt to miss the
ng, slow, unrecorded forces of population and tech-
ological changes, and even the development of eco-
omic and domestic institutions, which lie somewhere
low the level of the interests of chroniclers. By con-
ast, the Marxist, with his excessive emphasis on dia-
ctic, on class structure and economic interpretations
history, is apt to overlook the importance of non-
alectical cumulative processes of growth of knowl-
ge and technology. He is likely to underestimate
e significance of the autonomous dynamic processes
political, military, symbolic, and religious systems.
s any single model is almost by definition inadequate
d may therefore be misleading, there is much to be
id for the use of several different models and an
lectic frame of mind.

The use of quantification and of mathematical mod-
s needs special attention. The great advantage of
mbers is that they can be readily combined and
anipulated. Hence, if a particular phenomenon can
reduced to a numerical form, it is very easy to con-
nse large and confusing masses of information into a
gle index or figure. A good example of this would
the concept of the gross national product, which,

with all its weaknesses, is an enormously useful tool i
interpreting one of the large aggregate characteristi
of a society. We are able to use it because certain a
pects of social life, i.e., those connected with produ
tion, consumption, and exchange, are capable of fair
easy quantification. This is so because a price structu
exists from which we can derive valuation coefficien
that reduce an enormous heterogeneous mass of sho
and ships and sealing wax to a uniform number
dollars'-worth. The process of the quantification of hi
torical data is still in its infancy, and I believe ver
important modifications of our image of the past wi
emerge from it. Nevertheless, there should be a no
of warning. Like any other process of abstractio
quantification introduces into the information proces
ing operation a certain bias in favor of precisely thos
elements that can easily be quantified. Ease of quant
fication, however, is not necessarily closely related
the importance of a phenomenon in terms of the who
historical process. It is very hard, for instance, to app
quantification to symbolic systems, or to the dynami
of ethical and religious belief. Yet these systems ha
a life and dynamic of their own, and history certain
cannot be interpreted without them.

To return to the main question, let us consider ho
far it is possible to develop an abstract description c
the movement through time of a social system, in th
case a large society. The first problem is that of sta
description, i.e., how do we develop a means of de
scribing the state of a society at a given moment i
terms at once sufficiently simple and adequately rich
Total description is obviously impossible. To describ
the state of even a small society like Iceland or th
Maldive Islands, would require volumes enough to fi
all the libraries in the world. We must use some kin

f sampling methods to select information; in order to
ample we must have a universe from which to do so.
ncidentally, one of the great advantages of area sampling is that the spatial universe is usually fairly well
nown. For most countries we have reasonably adequate maps, and a map is a beginning of any state de-
cription.

The next universe is the human population itself.
Here the census is important in establishing the universe from which later samples may be made; for some
purposes, perhaps, area sampling can take the place of
a census. Even when we look at the human population,
however, the crucial question remains how much we
vant to know about it. Information collection is an economic problem. It exhibits in a marked degree the
phenomenon associated with scarcity. If we find out
one thing, we will not find out another. It is relatively
easy, although problematic, to find out a respondent's
ocation, age, marital status, family status, etc. It is
nore difficult, though still possible, to learn his re-
igious affiliations, his political preferences, and some-
hing of his range of vision in time and space. Things
hard to assimilate into the information system in any
quantitative way may be called the general character
variables. The F-scale, as a measurement of authori-
arianism, was an attempt to do something along these
ines, but we do not have any very good theory about
hese variables; even if we did, getting at them would
require long interviews of a kind which are impossible
n census enumeration.

One should perhaps visualize an orderly system of
nformation collection, beginning with a complete cen-
us for what might be called the basic universes; then
descending successively to smaller samples and longer
nterviews, finally to extensive depth interviews with a

relatively small sample of the population. An informa
tion collection process of this kind should also reveal :
great deal about the social structures of the society. I
would certainly yield information about organizationa
activity and organizations, about lines of communica
tion, e.g., who communicates with whom. It should
also be informative about population and the use o
artifacts, the non-human material objects interactin;
with human beings, e.g., farms, machines, newspapers
radios, automobiles, etc.

One of the major problems intrinsic to the process o
information collection is that of fitting the existin;
channels and previously gathered information into the
over-all picture. A considerable amount of the norma
activity of any society is devoted to collecting an
processing information. One thinks of accounting, lega
records, and the vast accumulation of documents com
mon to any reasonably literate society. Most records
however, are kept for particular purposes and are no
conceived of as part of a wider sample. By the nex
generation, thanks to the development of compute
technology, we may well have developed a universal
ized system of information collection and processing
Such a system would have profound implications fo
political and personal life, in terms of problems o
privacy, rights of access to knowledge, and so on. Ac
tually, these implications are already evident.

Once we have achieved a reasonably satisfactor
state description, the next task is to detect reasonabl
stable processes of state change. Most of these are
processes of consumption and production. All state.
of any system are consumptive, i.e., they depreciate
and decay. Persons age and die; capital depreciate:
and is exhausted. Knowledge is forgotten and in any
case is lost with death; foodstuffs are consumed, etc

These processes are usually governed by functions of the state itself. Thus, if age-specific death rates are stable, the over-all death rate is a function of the age distribution. A society composed of a large proportion of young people will have a low death rate; one having a large number of old people will have a high death rate. Food requirements of the human population are based on the fact that the human being burns up a certain amount of biological fuel and uses up certain amounts of protein and fat in the course of living. Corresponding to these processes of consumption—and largely induced by them—are the processes of production, which may be arbitrarily divided into processes that simply replace the consumption and restore the state to some initial condition, and processes that go beyond mere maintenance and raise the state itself to some higher level. Therefore, the dynamic state of the system largely depends on the excess of production over consumption. If births exceed deaths, the population will grow. If the production of goods exceeds their consumption, the capital stock will increase. If the gain in knowledge as a result of education and other information processes exceeds the loss of knowledge due to aging and death, a society's total stock of knowledge will increase. These are the most fundamental processes underlying the dynamic changes within the state. If they are fairly stable and especially if they are functionally related to the state itself, predictions can be made about the course of future events with some reasonable degree of probability.

We must, however, be alert to possible changes in rates of production and consumption, and changes in the functions relating the state to these rates. Population prediction has often been very unsuccessful because based on faulty assumptions about rates of change, or changes in rates. In the mid-1940s, for instance, the United States Bureau of the Census was still making projections of the population that proved to be considerably underestimated with the advent of a quite unexpected and persistent jump in the birth rate after 1947. In view of the information available at earlier periods, this change can quite reasonably be regarded as a random shift in the parameters of the system. Perhaps if we had known a little more about human motivation and the relation of birth rates to income, our projections might have been more accurate.

Similarly, in economic development, a society sometimes seems to operate according to a step-function, and quite suddenly adopts new rates of production and consumption, or savings and investment. There is, perhaps, something inherently unpredictable about these step-changes. Hence, whenever systems are liable to step-change, we should avoid confusing *projections* that do not allow for that liability with *predictions* that must allow for it if they are to be useful. Sometimes these step-changes are reversible, but more often seem irreversible; they represent what I have elsewhere called a systems break. This is a most intractable kind of phenomenon to interpret in terms of the dynamics of social systems. It is particularly significant, of course, in revolutionary changes, which accounts for the difficulty of predicting revolution.

There is a whole class of related phenomena that may be called "threshold systems," which operate successfully and predictably with a set of given parameters as long as these all lie within a certain range, or inside a given threshold. However, if any one of them goes beyond that threshold, irreversible processes set in that may result in profound system change. The death of a living organism is perhaps the

ost striking example of a threshold system: once a
ertain boundary is crossed, the homeostatic processes
f the system disintegrate and even its physical strucure soon decays and disappears. A less extreme case
ould be described as transfiguration, in which the
ystem, while retaining a certain identity through time,
; so reorganized as to be virtually unrecognizable.
ometimes these processes of transfiguration are im-
licit in the dynamics of the system itself, as in the
etamorphosis of a caterpillar into a butterfly, or an
gg into a chicken. In social systems these transforma-
ons may be more random, as for instance in the trans-
ormation of the character of a firm. (The company
at now produces Black Label Beer was originally a
roducer of mangles and then of automobiles, before
developed its present industry.) Similarly a Con-
regational Church may transform itself into a Uni-
arian one, and a state may have a Communist revolu-
ion. It is these uncertain transfigurations around which
much social conflict develops. Thus, it is both the
ncertainty and apparent irreversibility of the Com-
unist revolution that accounts for much of the emo-
ional intensity it has engendered.

It is sometimes possible to detect continuous changes
f a variable toward some recognizable threshold or
risis level, beyond which irreversible parametric
hange in the system will take place, either death or
ransfiguration. Doctors, for instance, identify the state
f a sick person as "critical," in which the variables of
is system are moving toward the irreversible bound-
ry of death, or "out of danger," in which the homeo-
tatic processes have reasserted themselves and the
rocess toward the death boundary has been reversed.
n the case of societies, soil erosion, increase in popula-
ion density in limited agricultural areas, and erosion

of ideologies or systems of legitimation, are example
of continuous processes which may lead to discontinu
ous thresholds. On the other hand, discontinuous
processes, certain one-shot events, profoundly change
the subsequent parameters of a social system. The
introduction of a road, a school, a mission, newspaper
circulation or electronic communication, may not represent any simple continuous pattern, yet may lead to
system breaks in the dynamic processes.

A very difficult question is that of the importance of
"key roles" in the society. Occasionally the death or
removal of someone in such a key role, like Stalin, produces quite large changes in the subsequent dynamic
of the society. However, there seem to be some societies, like those of Latin America, in which the latent
and continuous forces are so strong that no role occupant seems to affect the dynamics of the society in any
profound sense. The importance of key roles no doubt
depends to a considerable extent on the nature of the
societal power structure. In a pluralistic society with
many centers of power, the removal of a particular
role occupant makes less difference than it does in one
where all the channels of power lead to a single figure
at the top. It would be hard, for instance, to imagine
any change in Protestantism, with its highly pluralistic
organization, comparable in rapidity and magnitude
with the changes introduced in the Roman Catholic
Church by the late Pope John XXIII. Clearly, it should
be possible to define and even to measure the significance of social role, but up to now it has been given
little serious attention.

One phenomenon often overlooked is the structure
and historical succession of age roles in a society. Thus,
in Japan, a rebellious and radical role is quite accepta-
ble for the student, and the casual observer might con-

clude therefore that the country will move sharply to the left when the present student generation comes to maturity and power. If, however, there is inherent in the society a specific role for youthful rebellion, if the general pattern is one of radical youth and conservative age, we should be wary of projecting the character of today's youth into the adult society of the next generation. Even so, it is also important to identify the operative influences on youth, for in many respects people do not much change as they get older; the experiences of youth often determine the attitudes of middle age. This is particularly apt to be true of traumatic experiences. The attitudes of the generation now administering the United States are so deeply colored by the Great Depression and Munich that it is almost impossible for this generation to be realistic about the contemporary world.

Changes in methods of child-rearing can have a profound long-range effect on the character of a population, and hence of a total society. Thus we should look for substantial changes in the character especially of the middle-class population of the United States, after the introduction of new child-rearing techniques between the 1930s and 1940s. Through the impact of his famous book on child-rearing, Dr. Spock may well be the most influential American of the twentieth century. We must also study very carefully the shift from family to nursery school, especially in socialist societies, and the possible impact of this on the character of the rising generation. Everett Hagen[1] bases his long-run dynamics essentially on the slow transformation of the parent-child relationship as the traditional society is threatened and invaded by ideas and people and arti-

[1] Everett E. Hagen, *On the Theory of Social Change* (Homewood, Ill.: The Dorsey Press, 1962).

facts from the developed world. This suggestion is highly plausible, but we still do not know enough about the dynamics of personality growth and change to estimate the relative importance of, say, childhood influences, influences in adolescence, and the learning processes of later life.

Perhaps the element of the social system least reducible to simple models and a trustworthy information process is the symbolic, i.e., the symbols, ideas, ideologies, theologies, myths, etc., that constitute the basis of community and around which develop deep passions and strongly held values. Most of the destructive and protracted conflicts besetting society have their origin in symbolic systems. Conflicts of interest can usually be adjusted by some bargaining process; but because they strike so deeply at the personal identity and self-image of the individual, and at the basis of community itself, conflicts of faith and ideology are extremely hard to resolve.

One of the most puzzling phenomena of history is the occasional outbreak of what might be called "symbolic epidemics"—the rise of a new religion or a new political ideology or even a new nationalism. Phenomena like the spread of Christianity or of Islam or of Communism or even of science and the world superculture exhibit many of the characteristics of biological epidemics, and it is by no means easy to identify the conditions under which they will take hold and be successful. The contagion of ideas, as far as I know, is something which has rarely been studied at the level of the total society, though there have been many studies of individual conversion. Epidemiological theory suggests that this is a phenomenon where again there are critical values of certain variables, such as the contagiousness, above which a contagion will spread among large populations and below which it will recede and reach a low-level equilibrium. What it is, however, that makes certain ideas contagious is something about which we understand very little. A study of the relative success of a rather constant missionary effort in different countries, such as that of the Mormons, would be extremely interesting.

In all these processes we can detect two major elements. One might be called the non-human element in the social system, involving such things as climatic changes, bacteriological mutations, soil erosion, etc. The second element in the system, the human element, is almost wholly concerned with the process of human learning, involving the rise or decline or transformation of the total stock of human knowledge. Up to this point in the development of the social sciences, learning has been treated largely on an individual basis. The time now seems to be ripe for the development both of theoretical systems and of empirical studies of learning on the scale of the large society, or what might be called the "macrolearning" process. The events of each day are impressed on the memories of the participants, and so add to the total structure of knowledge where the impact is positive, or subtract from it through denial, forgetting, aging, and death. If we could find some fairly simple analytical structure to portray this process, we would be far advanced toward solving the problem of the dynamics of total societies. It is not inconceivable that we might sample the information output of a particular day and employ a set of weights relating the information output to changes in the knowledge structure, or in the sum total of images of the world held by the population. We might then be able to find important clues to the more continuous and on-going processes by which the knowledge structure is changed. Then, as ever, of course we would have to be on the lookout for the step-functions and the discontinuities and system breaks. With all the difficulties, however, some genuine knowledge of the dynamics of total societies seems to be possible.

Perhaps the greatest problem in developing knowledge about total societies is the sheer difficulty, expense, and political sensitivity involved in setting up an adequate process of collecting information. Once information is collected, we have fairly good methods for processing it and interpreting it. Many of the fundamental difficulties of the social sciences, however, arise from the fact that their basic data are collected largely as by-products of other activities such as taxation, customs collection and migration restrictions. Even though an increasing amount of information is collected purely out of curiosity, it still represents a small proportion of the total. We also face the difficulty that the very collection of information and the development of knowledge about social systems is itself part of the systems, and is likely to be a crucial element in their dynamics. All decisions are made on the basis of some image of the world derived from some form of information processing. If, therefore, we introduce the collection and processing of social scientific information into the social system, we cannot expect it to remain unchanged, and the political sensitivity of such information collection and processing depends on this fact. We have been fairly successful in collecting and processing economic data on the scale of the total society, as the development of national income statistics proves. If we can structure the process on a regular, systematic, month-by-month basis for other essential social variables, it will constitute an enormous step forward towards a viable social science. I have suggested that we require a network of social data stations, analogous perhaps to the meteorological stations collecting data about the atmosphere. Without such a network, it is hard to see how really substantial knowledge collection processes about the "sociosphere" can be developed. This is probably a task for the United Nations rather than for any merely national agency, because the collection of knowledge, like any other social process, has to be legitimated if it is to be continuous. The experience with Project Camelot illustrates the difficulty of legitimating any major information collection and processing operation merely through the agency of national institutions. It is the basic illegitimacy of the nation-state itself outside its own borders that is the real problem; a world system of social data collection and processing must be legitimated by world organizations.

ANATOL RAPOPORT

MATHEMATICAL, EVOLUTIONARY, AND PSYCHOLOGICAL APPROACHES TO THE STUDY OF TOTAL SOCIETIES

The social scientist is frequently torn between a compulsion to emulate the established prestige-endowed "hard" sciences with their paraphernalia of data-processing and mathematical machinery, on the one hand, and on the other, a longing to bring "intuitive understanding" to bear upon the study of man. An approach which, I believe, makes possible a social science which can be both imaginatively creative and "hard" is the so-called system-theoretic approach. An abstract theory of systems (general system theory) makes possible the study of organized complexity and for this reason seems especially promising for the study of whole societies. Ideas of general system theory stem partly from mathematics, partly from technology, and partly from biology. In what follows I shall pass over only briefly the mathematical approach, which has been amply treated elsewhere, and, omitting the technological approach, shall develop some ideas rooted in the biological approach.

Mathematically speaking a portion of the world can be called a system if (1) at any given time the "state" of this portion can be described by a set of values assigned to some selected set of variables, and (2) relations of interdependence can be ascribed to the variables. If, in addition, knowledge of the values of the variables at some initial time and knowledge of the relations among the variables allows us to predict (deterministically or probabilistically) the state of the system at some arbitrary future time, we have a dynamic theory of the system. If we can infer only the values of some of the variables from those of others at a specified moment of time, we have a static theory.

Mathematical physics deals both with static and dynamic theories of systems. For example, a gas confined in a volume constitutes a system. If equilibrium has been reached, the volume, the temperature, and the pressure exerted by the gas upon the walls of the container are the three variables which describe the state of the system. These three variables are interrelated, because knowledge of any two of them implies knowledge of the third. In other words, the three variables are connected by an equation which constitutes the static theory of the system.

The theory of the motions of heavenly bodies is a dynamic one. The state of this system at any moment of time is given by specifying the positions and the velocities of all the bodies comprising it. The equations of motion and the law of gravity enable us to determine all the future positions and velocities, i.e., all the future states if an initial state is given. These equations therefore constitute a dynamic theory.

Another example of a system is an automaton with a repertoire of "states." The action of the environment upon such a system is called the input to the system. If the automaton is a deterministic one, then the input at any given moment—together with the state of the automaton—determines an output and the next state. Knowledge of these relations enables us to predict the successive states of the automaton and also its output, once we know the input.

We can in principle conceptualize a "total society"

in this way. It is assumed that a model of this sort with any pretense to verisimilitude would be one of overwhelming complexity. It is unlikely that a tractable theory of total societies could be developed by examining models of this sort because we could not hope to hit on the "right" model from the start; it would be impractical to proceed by trial and error simply because a complete examination of each model would take too long. Nevertheless, automaton models of society have a certain heuristic value. They accustom us to think in terms of certain concepts which may be relevant to the study of total societies. For example, we can imagine that a society has a repertoire of "states." We can also imagine that it is acted upon by the environment (events impinging on the society from the outside) and that these events together with concurrent states of the system determine both the succeeding states and the output, i.e., the reaction of the system to the inputs.

It should be clear that the character of the system is immaterial for a general system theory, at least with regard to the conceptualization just described. The system can be a single organism, a part of the organism (for example, the brain or the digestive system), a collection of organisms (for example, a family, a city, an institution), or a nation, or an entire species, such as the human race. Although in practice we cannot hope to even list all the "states" of such systems, much less indicate the relations among variables which determine a state or a progression of states, the conceptualization is useful because it distinguishes problems to be seized.

The most straightforward application of such methods is in those areas where aspects of the system can be readily described in terms of quantifiable variables.

The economy of a nation is an example. An economy can be pictured as a system of flow. Raw materials are obtained from natural resources or are imported. They undergo transformations into various products, which, in turn, undergo further transformations, and so on, until some final product is consumed. The rate of transformation of one product into another implies a rate of increase of the second at the expense of the first. Besides, there are "sources," i.e., rates of entry of products into the system, and "sinks," rates of exit from the system. In this way, the entire economy can in principle be represented by a so-called flow matrix. From the study of such a matrix, one can infer the effects upon the system of changes in any of its components, for example, the effects of a technological change that, if utilized, may alter the rate of transformation of one product into another, with repercussions throughout the system.

Another example, considerably simpler than that of the total economy, is the age composition of the population. Here all that is required is the age composition at some initial time, plus birth and age-specific death rates, plus age-specific immigration and emigration rates, if these are important. If the above mentioned rates are constant or known as functions of time, the age composition of the population can be calculated for any future time, as long as the specified rates remain in force. Geographical distributions can be studied in the same way if rates and directions of flow of populations are known. These phenomena are the subject matter of demography.

So far we have been considering isolated aspects, each within the province of a special discipline, e.g., economics or demography. Conceivably, however, we could "build up" a science of a total society by com-

bining various aspects. For example, demographic phenomena are clearly related to economic ones. For
one thing, the state of economy may influence the geo-
graphic distribution of the population, which, in turn,
has a bearing on the flow system of economy (through
influence on the availability of labor and of consum-
ers). Thus the demographic and the economic systems,
being interdependent, can be conceived as a single
system. There is no theoretical limit to how far the
process of enlarging the scope of relevant aspects can
go.

The practical limitations are obviously severe. It
would be hopeless, for example, to treat the combined
demographic-economic model by classical analytic
methods. The only practical treatment is by computer
simulation. The limitations of this method are imposed
by the availability of computer technology and by the
state of refinement of this technology.

The approach just outlined follows the precepts of
the exact sciences in the sense that it puts at the center
of attention quantifiable variables and from their interrelations deduces conclusions about the possible states
of a social system or predictions about the succession
of such states in time (i.e., about the "trajectory" of the
system).

Mathematical models of this type derive their power
from the fact that once relations among variables are
specified, the resulting theory is quite independent of
the *content* of the variables. For example, it does not
matter whether we are studying the distribution of a
population according to age brackets, incomes, profes-
sions, or national origins. All we need to know is the
laws of the dynamic interrelations of the relevant variables. If two such sets of laws of interaction are isomorphic, so will be the resulting theories. The mathemati-

cal model is thus a great "unifier" of theories by virtue of the fact that it abstracts relations from content. Only relations enter into the making of a mathematical theory.

The limitations of mathematical models of real processes are obvious. Such models have predictive or explanatory power only if relevant variables can be clearly distinguished and if the relations among them are reasonable approximations to relations that actually obtain. Neither condition is likely to be satisfied in phenomena whose course is determined by factors not readily discernible, or where the interactions among relevant variables are of such complexity that they can not be readily formulated.

There are, however, other models of phenomena besides the precisely formulated mathematical models. Every model is an analogy: it describes a portion of the world in terms of relations presumed known. Historically, general system theory has been developed in part in the context of analogies drawn between biological and social phenomena. Such analogies were already offered in the Middle Ages. For the most part, they stemmed from naïve uses of metaphor, e.g., the kingship was represented by the head of an animal, the peasantry by the back, etc. Because of the long and largely sterile history of metaphorical analogies, the analogical method of theory construction has fallen into disrepute. It is not true, however, that the method is doomed to remain sterile. We have seen that mathematical analogy can be immensely fruitful, resting as it does not on metaphorical identification of impressions but on very real correspondences of structural relations between two or more objects or phenomena.

Between the rigorous analogies revealed by the mathematical models and the free-wheeling metaphorical analogies, there are analogies of an intermediate degree of rigor. These serve as the building blocks of the so-called organismic general system theory.

An organismic system theory takes its cue from certain features common to all living systems. Proceeding from the assumption that a living system is in the first instance a complex organized entity, organismic general system theory proceeds to list the essential features of such entities.

To begin with, organized complex entities (systems) consist of identifiable parts (subsystems or elements) which stand in specifiable relations to each other. These relations may be spatial (e.g., residing in the arrangement of the parts) or functional (e.g., described in terms of the *potential* effects of changes in some parts upon those of another). The primitive parts and the specified relations among them constitute the *structure* of the system. For example, the organizational chart of an institution, together with a specification of the operational meanings of the links indicating subordinate, superordinate, and co-ordinate relations, constitute the structure of the institution.

Next, a system responds to inputs from the environment and to inner changes. Short-term responses (of this sort which are to an extent reversible) constitute the laws of the system's behavior. An important class of such responses are those preserving an equilibrium or a steady state of some sort, such as the homeostatic mechanisms of physiological regulation in an organism and certain balance-preserving responses of an ecological system to not-too-severe changes in the environment.

Finally, a system undergoes certain long-term irreversible changes. In the case of an organism, these changes are manifested in the organism's embryological development, maturation, senescence, and death. In the case of biological species (which, in virtue of interbreeding patterns and ecological interrelations, can also be conceived as components of a system), these secular changes are manifested in evolution. In the case of a society, the secular changes constitute the history of a society.

There is a clear interdependence among the structural, functional, and evolutionary aspects of a system. Function is obviously dependent on structure. Through behavior, function determines the interaction of the system with its environment and so the "fate" of the system, i.e., its history. In the case of evolution, the components of evolutionary change, i.e., mutation pressures, selection pressures, etc., determine, in turn, the structure and therefore the function of the evolving systems.

The correspondences between the mathematical and the organismic approaches to general system theory are easy to discern. If a system is represented by a mathematical model, e.g., the flow matrix of an economy, or by demographic equations, then the structure of the system is reflected in the network of interdependence among the variables of the model. The behavior of the system is represented, perhaps, by departures from the equilibria or from the steady states and by return to such states. The evolution of the system is represented by the slower, long-run secular trends toward new equilibrium configurations.

The difference between organismic and mathematical models is that the latter are more rigorous and precise while the former are, in certain instances, more richly suggestive.

The suggestiveness of a model resides in the analogies it draws. For example, it is known that living systems, in the process of maintaining a homeostatic equilibrium, mobilize defenses against invading foreign bodies. Inorganic foreign bodies may be encapsulated or expelled. Organic foreign bodies may be destroyed by antibodies. However, just because societies exhibit some characteristics of living systems, in particular homeostatic characteristics, it would be rash to assume that every process found in the organism has an analogue in society. Such expectations would be symptomatic of naïve analogizing, characteristic of prescientific speculations about natural phenomena. However, there is another way of looking for analogies between organisms and societies. Both are clearly instances of organized complexity. We know that forces are always operating upon such systems and tend to disorganize them. This is the Second Law of Thermodynamics in its most general formulation. The fact that, for a time at least, systems do maintain their status as organized complexities suggests that their continued existence is a consequence of their having developed defenses against disorganizing influences. Therefore it seems worthwhile to look for the specific mechanisms by which these defenses are maintained.

We do find, in fact, that every society has a certain tolerance for deviant members in its midst and certain ways of dealing with them when the deviance passes beyond the limits of tolerance. These defense mechanisms against internal threats are universally observed in all systems resembling organisms in some fundamental respect, including human and non-human groups.

Principles of evolution through natural selection are another example of universal principles operating in complex systems. Even artifacts made by human beings evolve according to principles of natural selection. Observe the evolution of the automobile from the carriage, a classical example of technological evolution. The example is remarkable in that even such features as vestigial parts are observed in the early models of the automobile. Those early versions still had sockets in which whips were inserted on carriages. The gradual change of shape of the automobile, the elimination of superfluous parts like the running board, the adaptation of the engine to the changes in fuel, etc., all are manifestations of true evolution.

There is little doubt that the principles operating in the evolution of societies are very much like the principles of organic evolution. It is not necessary to invoke any mystical or metaphysical notions to subscribe to this view, as did Goethe, Lamarck and Bergson, the "romantic" exponents of evolution. Natural selection is a simple, extremely "prosaic" principle, and it acts without distinction on biological, technological, and social phenomena. Even topographical features can be often explained in terms of "natural selection," for example, the arrangement of pebbles according to their sizes along the water line of a beach. The regular gradation from fine to coarse is a result of differential rates at which the pebbles are dropped by the wave that carries them.

An example of an evolving system intermediate between the organic and the inorganic is strikingly instructive. Termites, as is known, build elaborate dwellings. The architectural plan of these dwellings is characteristic of the species, i.e., the layout of the galleries, etc., is actually part of the termite's genetic heritage. Each generation builds like the previous one, not because they copy the plan (as we humans do) but because they cannot build otherwise. In fact, none of the termites building a nest has ever seen a termite nest before. The process of building the labyrinth is composed of innumerable tiny acts by each builder. These acts are responses of the individual insect to his situation. The pattern of responses is pre-programed in the insect's nervous system.

Although the genetic heritage determining the life pattern of a termite of a given species is remarkably stable, it is not absolutely so. From time to time, mutations occur, i.e., changes in the genes, which manifest themselves in somatic changes. These may be anatomical (e.g., sizes and shapes of organs), or physiological (changes in enzymes which, in turn, change the patterns of chemical reactions that constitute the physiological process of the insect). They may be "psychological" changes. In the case of the termite, these probably involve changes in the structure of its nervous system that make for somewhat different reactions to stimuli. Since the architectural plan of a termite "city" is the result of the totality of reactions to stimuli produced by the army of builders, it follows that mutations in the termite result in changes in the architectural plan.

Actually the chain of events is even longer. For the genetic changes occur not in the builders themselves— the sexless workers, who do not reproduce—but in the reproducing individuals, who do not work. We have, thus, the following chain. Genetic changes in the reproducing individuals result in a somewhat altered "psychology" of all their progeny, i.e., the whole termite colony. The altered psychology results in somewhat different patterns of actions constituting building activity. The sum total of these changes in the patterns of building behavior results in a somewhat altered architectural plan of the termite city. Consequently, the *termite city* (which is not a living organism but merely an ossified trace of the activity of living organisms) *also evolves.* Indeed, we can trace the evolution of a termite city as clearly as the evolution of the species itself. We can see evidences of specific mutations and even such things as vestigial features. For example, galleries that lead nowhere and are apparently useless have been shown to be instances of biological obsolescence. Thousands or millions of years ago these galleries were functional. Their function has been lost, but the now useless passages have remained in much the same way that we have retained our vermiform appendix and the early horseless carriages featured whip sockets.

Evidence of entirely analogous phenomena among human beings are plentiful. The clearest examples are found in English spelling. To the child learning to spell, and even to his teacher whose only concern is to inculcate reading and writing skills, words like knife, knight, colonel, and quiz are a nuisance. Life would be simpler if we could write with impunity nife, nite, kernel, and kwiz. The reason we do not is clear: knife used to be canif; knight used to be knecht; colonel is pronounced *colonel* in French; quiz is related to question, inquiry, and all the other words, in which the idea of interrogation is manifested in the letter *q*. Thus we have an understandable desire to have a written language reflecting our spoken language as faithfully as possible; but we also have the force of tradition, sometimes bolstered by a need to preserve some ideographic features in the written language (for example, in scientific terms like Psychology, Dynamics, Science, etc. This conservative force resists the tendency toward the phonetization of the written language. The actual evolution of spelling manifests itself in a compromise between the two forces.

In evolving societies, vestigial institutions are often

no less conspicuous. Some of these institutions remain viable by assuming a different social function, e.g., the royal dynasties of northern European democracies. Others persist even though they may be widely recognized as obsolete or dysfunctional, e.g., certain tariffs, some fiscal policies, and the military establishments of militarily indefensible states.

These examples illustrate the formidable explanatory power of the evolutionary point of view. The existence of apparently useless features in the termite nest and apparently senseless features of English spelling, is definitely explained if (1) the nest and the language are seen in historical perspective, and (2) if something is known about evolutionary mechanisms. Note that (1) alone is not sufficient. Suppose that the termite nest is seen in historical perspective but that the observer is committed to the Lamarckian view of evolution. According to this view, evolution results from the supposed fact that each generation "strives" toward a greater adaptation to environment and from the supposed transmission of the resultant changes to successive generations. Thus, to quote the classical Lamarckian explanation, the giraffe has come by his long neck as a result of "stretching" on the part of individual giraffes as they reached for leaves on trees. In the process of stretching, the necks grew longer and each generation of giraffes had slightly longer necks than their parents. This explanation becomes untenable in the face of the evolution of social insects like ants, bees, and termites. For the workers of these species (in which the experience is supposed to accumulate), being sexless, have no progeny. Whatever transmissible changes occur must occur in the kings and queens, who do *not* have the relevant experiences.

Once this is understood, the non-functional features

in the life of organisms (for example, useless galleries) are seen to be not anomalies or accidents but necessary consequences of the evolutionary process.

Similarly, it is not enough to know that the k in "know" is there because the word is related to older Germanic forms (in which it was functional). We also must know why vestigial written features are preserved. Here we can only make guesses, because our understanding of the mechanisms of cultural evolution does not compare with our understanding of the mechanisms of biological evolution. We can be convinced, however, that such mechanisms exist, just as the early evolutionists were convinced that mechanisms of biological evolution existed. Indeed the search for these mechanisms has made biology the almost unified science it has become. Biology is well on the way to becoming the "science of all life" by virtue of the links that have been established between taxonomy and genetics, between genetics and physiology, and between physiology and ecology.[1] The system-theoretical point of view has played a part in this process by providing the necessary "cognitive set" which emphasized the interdependence of the various aspects of life, rather than the specialized aspects studied in the traditional disciplines or the special forms of life emphasized in classical "natural history."

It seems that in the study of total societies a system-oriented "cognitive set" is also necessary. This does not mean a return to the vague formulations of the roman-

[1] The subject matter of ecology is the interaction of populations in a common environment. Viewed as a system, a biological community can be considered as a superorganism with its own "chain of metabolism," regulatory mechanisms, etc. Thus the ecological interrelations (e.g., predator-prey relations, symbiosis, etc.) can be viewed as the "physiology" of the superorganism.

ticists. To apply the holistic view in a scientific context, one should start with circumscribed problems like those chosen by the geneticists in their efforts to uncover the mechanisms of evolution.

The evolution of spelling or, somewhat more generally, the evolution of language is an example of such a problem. The fact of evolution of language is unquestionable and has already been recognized by the "romantic" evolutionists. What, however, are the mechanisms? This is the scientific problem. In the search for such mechanisms, we shall be led to investigate the ways in which language habits are transmitted, the factors favoring conservation of such habits and those creating pressures for change; also the mechanisms of language "interbreeding," the processes of speciation, maturation, senescence, and extinction. Obviously the physical bases of these mechanisms are entirely different from those of biological evolution, but their interactive effects may well exhibit striking analogies. This leads us to suppose that there are even more general laws of evolution of which biological and linguistic evolutionary processes are special manifestations.

What shall we have accomplished in such a study toward creating a science of "total societies"? We shall have gained experience in conducting investigations which, there is reason to hope, will lay the foundations of such a science. For example, the repertoire of concepts derived from biological evolution constitutes a cognitive set for studying other evolutionary phenomena. Studies of evolutions other than organic will enlarge this conceptual repertoire and will put already existing concepts into a more general context. They will alert the investigators both to the opportunities inherent in drawing significant analogies and to the dangers of pressing superficial ones too far.

Once we have acquired experience of the sort described, we can move on to studies more directly related to the theory of total society, e.g., the study of institutions from the evolutionary point of view.

Here I must digress in order to evaluate two different and occasionally competitive methods in the study of cultures and societies. I have already described the one that emphasizes historical perspective. In the nineteenth century this method was used by social thinkers who, however, lacked reliable knowledge about the mechanisms of social change. Throughout the nineteenth century, evolution was practically identified with "progress," and progress was assumed to be inherent in the nature of history. Thus in the early decades of the century, Hegel built his theory of social evolution on a purely metaphysical principle of the unfolding of an Idea. Toward the middle of the century, Marx proposed a more specific mechanism of social change, namely the class struggle. Therefore, disregarding the degree of validity of Marx's assumptions and conclusions, his theory of the total society was developed in a scientific mode, in the sense that it is based on specific and, in part, demonstrable hypotheses. Toward the turn of the century, Lewis H. Morgan viewed the evolution of society as a clear lineal progression through well-defined stages: savagery, barbarism, civilization. Common to all these writers was the characteristic nineteenth-century idea of progress. Evolution, for them, was a growth, an unfolding of potentialities.

A rival view, the so-called functionalist model of social institutions, was introduced in the first half of the twentieth century. This approach de-emphasized or altogether ignored historical perspectives. The basic datum in the functionalist model is a cross section of a society at a given time. The problem is to discover how the various "parts" of this cross section, e.g., the institutions, patterns of life, thinking habits, etc., fit together. It is assumed that each of the "parts" is there because it serves some purpose in keeping the society viable.

Note that in many ways the progressive evolutionary and the functionalist views will yield altogether different interpretations of observed societal characteristics. Thus the progressive evolutionary view assumed that societies in the state of "barbarism" have simply not yet attained the state of "civilization." Such an interpretation is inadmissible in the functionalist view, which examines various societal institutions and life patterns only with reference to their manner of adaptation to their actual environment and (most important) to each other.

It is easy to see how the functionalist view arose as a reaction to the progressive-evolutionary view of society. It originated among the cultural anthropologists who, in their studies of so-called "primitive" societies, developed a considerable "empathy" toward ways of living and thinking that appeared simply backward to the uninitiated. The empathy was not necessarily rooted in sentiment (although sentiment might have played a part). It arose, rather, as a necessary component of the cultural anthropologist's methods. The anthropologist gets a large portion of his data from so-called "informants," i.e., native respondents. To stimulate the flow of information, a certain rapport must be established between the investigator and the informant. The anthropologists discovered that they could begin to understand certain aspects of the life they were studying only if they learned to empathize.

This discovery is especially pertinent to the study of "exotic" languages. It is impossible to pursue such studies systematically if one insists on imposing upon every language preconceived notions of linguistic structure. Once the barrier of linguistic ethnocentrism was breached, the notion that the languages of "primitive people" were "primitive" had to be abandoned. These languages were revealed to be as sophisticated and complex as Latin and English. What appeared as "illogical" in the "primitive" languages was now seen to be entirely "logical" in the light of different structural principles. Paucity in certain respects was seen to be amply compensated for by richness in other respects. Thus the notion that language is subject to some sort of lineal "progressive" evolutionary development had to be abandoned, as were other ideas of lineal progressive social evolution. Functional anthropologists preferred to see each society as an organic whole to be described and explained in terms of its own coherence and adaptation to its own environment. In a way the functionalist view was a rejection of Western ethnocentrism, which, in its crude form, regarded the Papuans and the Hottentots as embryonic or retarded Europeans.

Can the functionalist view of society be reconciled with an evolutionary view? It can, if one important assumption is made, namely that the equilibrium, which, in the functionalist view, is being maintained within a society and between the society and its environment, has been attained through the evolutionary process. This assumption is frequently justified in the biological context. Consider an organism like a mosquito or a cactus plant. The functionalist's problem is to discover the functions served by the organism's anatomical, physiological, and behavioral characteristics. Why does an organism have a given shape? What role does a given chemical reaction play in the digestive process? How is survival of the individual or the species served by a given behavior pattern? The answers are frequently convincing; it turns out that the characteristics of an organism are just about what they ought to be if it is to survive in its environment. Moreover, the characteristics are adapted not only to the environment but to each other. The mosquito's equipment for piercing skin is coupled with its equipment for gorging itself on blood and digesting the blood quickly.

If the mosquito is seen to be the end result of an evolutionary process, which is assumed to tend toward an equilibrium, the functional meaning of the mosquito's equipment can be supposed to be a manifestation of evolution. Thus the functionalist can claim that his view of society is reconcilable with an evolutionary view. It is only necessary to suppose that the existing societies are end products of an evolutionary process.

At one time, the appropriately equipped organism was considered providential. During the "romantic" period of evolutionary theory (Goethe, Lamarck), the approach was in terms of "strivings," etc. At present, natural selection is the accepted biological theory. The adapted organisms exist because the non-adapted ones do not. This implies that non-adapted organisms occasionally exist, but do not survive. Moreover, a given line of descent, after a long period of existence, may become extinct when it is no longer adapted. Therefore, after a long period of lineal adaptation there must be a short period during which a non-adapted form exists, on borrowed time as it were.

If a functionalist theory of society is to be linked with an evolutionary one, then some analogical mechanism of evolution must be proposed. If we discount divine Providence and the romantic Lamarckian notions (which in the cultural context become variants of nationalist mystique), we are led again to natural selection as the only plausible mechanism. But now we see why an argument for cultural functionalism based on a natural selection principle is shaky. The analogy with biological adaptation cannot be made, because the "number of cultures" is exceedingly small compared to the number of genotypes or even to the number of species upon which natural selection is operating. Moreover, the time spans in which we measure cultural history are incomparably shorter than those applicable to the history of a species: biological evolution is exceedingly slow by historical standards. For this reason, biological evolution seems to pass through a sequence of equilibrium states. Departures from equilibrium are comparatively so transient (on the biological time scale) that they tend not to be noticed in the total process. Cultural evolution, however, takes place on the historical scale. It can indeed be seen, especially in our day of exceedingly rapid changes. Hence it is reasonable to suppose that none of the existing cultures is in equilibrium with its environment. There may have been such instances, when societies were virtually isolated for long periods of time; but those societies are precisely the ones that in recent times have been undergoing the most rapid developmental changes (e.g., Japan) or are on their way to extinction (e.g., Amerindian tribal societies and, possibly, Tibet).

In view of the unlikelihood that "cultural equilibrium" exists anywhere in the world today, the functionalist view has a weak theoretical basis. "Functional" institutions, i.e., those which contribute to the viability of a society, may rapidly become dysfunctional.

For this reason it would appear that although, in the biological context, we may derive a functionalist view of an organism from an evolutionary one, we cannot do so in the social or cultural context: "natural selection," which in its biological context is the force that establishes equilibrium by eliminating dysfunctional features, does not have time to operate in the cultural context.

The problem, therefore, is to create a dynamic (non-equilibrium) theory of social evolution. It is somewhat analogous to a corresponding problem in thermodynamics, and may be instructively examined in that context. Classical thermodynamics should properly be called thermostatics, because the systems considered in that theory are always assumed to be in equilibrium, internally and with the environment. When a system changes state, it is supposed to move through a sequence of equilibria, i.e., so slowly that equilibrium is being constantly re-established. In the last three or four decades, "thermodynamic" theory has been extended to cover non-equilibrium states, i.e., has begun to justify its name. As any physicist will testify, the genuinely dynamic theory is incomparably more difficult than the classical theory.

A functional theory of a total society is analogous to thermostatics. What we need is an extension to a dynamic theory where the assumption of the "adaptive equilibrium" is dropped. Such an approach would be evolutionary, but the natural selection principle based on the stability of *adaptive* characteristics would be replaced by one related to natural selection but not necessarily in its *adaptive* form. It is unnecessary (indeed not permissible) to assume that societal institutions, patterns of life, etc., exist because they contribute to societal viability. They may well be the seeds of the society's destruction, but this does not necessarily preclude their selection and fixation in societal evolution.

What can we assume, then, in place of the classical natural selection principle which guarantees the "survival of the fittest"? Here we are distinctly in the world of conjecture. For the time being, we cannot confine our theorizing to either the analysis of hard data or to the construction of models on rigorous deductive bases, as is done with mathematical models. We must rely on imagination and insight. Some illumination is provided by psychologists, semanticists, and others concerned with language and symbols as fundamental determinants of human behavior. They assume that human beings, unlike other animals, are in contact with their environment and with each other, not directly but via an intermediate "screen of language," i.e., it is not events that are the input to the human nervous system but the *meanings* of events. These meanings are not inherent in the events themselves, but are formed in the minds of the recipients as events are filtered through their cognitive sets. These cognitive sets, in turn, are transmitted from generation to generation. The transmission is effected not primarily through biological mechanisms (as with those animals whose patterns of behavior are "pre-programed"); nor are they learned anew by each generation (as with animals capable of learning from experience but not possessing a symbol language). They are transmitted from generation to generation by a process that would seem to be peculiar to our species. Alfred Korzybski chose the term "time-binding" to emphasize the fundamental distinction among plants, animals, and humans. He called plants "energy-binders," because their survival mechanism depends on their ability to capture energy from an external source (sunlight) and so to synthesize the compounds required for survival. He called animals "space-binders," because their motility enables them to seek out food, mates, and refuge. He called humans "time-binders," because our survival depends crucially on our ability to accumulate cultural (not only individual) experience. Time-binding is to culture what learning is to an organism, and what evolution is to a species. Boulding has proposed the term "macro-learning" to emphasize the learning aspects of cultural evolution.

Learning means selective accumulation of behavior patterns. Biological evolution is a selective accumulation of genes in an interbreeding population. The direction of learning, as well as the direction of evolution (biological and cultural), is determined by two factors: (1) adaptation to an environment or a situation, and (2) *what has already been accumulated*. Evolutionary improvement of the respiratory mechanism can take place only when the respiratory mechanism is present; improvement of locomotion depends on an efficient respiratory mechanism. Aviation could not develop without radio communication. National institutions cannot function without an internalized idea of "nationhood." Moreover, the dependence of one development on another goes both ways. In individual learning, skills reinforce interest, which, in turn, reinforces skills; in biological evolution, changes in structure give rise to changes in function, which, in turn, determine the direction of further structural changes; in culture evolution, institutional changes stimulate changes in social relations, which feed back into new institutional arrangements.

To understand cultural evolution scientifically means to uncover the mechanisms of time-binding. It is a matter of discovering what in the societal experience, considered organically, is meaningful and what is not, and, consequently, what gets admitted into the store of transmittable "knowledge" (the cultural "gene pool") and what does not.

The word "knowledge" is put in quotation marks advisedly, because the set of beliefs accumulated by time-binding may or may not be related to reality. Only a narrow sector of "knowledge" so accumulated can be said to reflect the real world. Today we call it scientific knowledge. It is related to the real world by virtue of the scientist's awareness of the language screen.

Science is a way of checking the objective bases of our beliefs (which in the scientific context are called "theories"). For the most part, we hold our beliefs because they fit into our cognitive set, not because they are related to reality. It is possible that belief systems, once established, develop according to their own dynamic laws and can come to dominate the whole fabric of life of a society *without having any necessary bearing on the real world.* When this happens to an individual, we call him psychotic. Sometimes it seems to us that whole societies become psychotic. In the absence of reliable knowledge about what governs the "psyche" of a society, the designation of a whole society as psychotic must remain a figure of speech. It is not particularly convincing and can be easily challenged. Yet there is no reason to ignore the possibility that societal psychosis may well be a subject of serious scientific investigation.

At least three recent instances come to mind. One was the psychosis which gripped the U.S.S.R. in the mid-thirties, as a result of which 90 per cent of Communist Party and military cadres were destroyed in the purges. This bloodletting might well have been fatal in the war that followed. Indeed, the outcome of the war hung in the balance for a year and a half. This precarious situation has been attributed to the decimation of technically competent and politically devoted personnel by Stalin—an act unexplainable except as a manifestation of a psychotic episode. Since the whole society participated in the act, the psychotic episode must be attributed to it.

A second example is the Nazi psychosis, which plunged Germany and the rest of the world into the most destructive war humanity had ever seen and which has probably planted the seeds of another holocaust, which humanity may not survive. If this happens, the conjecture offered above, to the effect that lasting institutions may well be maladaptive, will have been corroborated. The institution in question is the armed nation state.

The final example of societal psychosis is one that may be difficult for us to recognize, because we are engulfed by it. This is the anti-Communist fixation of present American foreign policy, which may make the extinction of the human race, or at least a return to a primitive state, inevitable. The symptoms are typical of psychosis: detachment from reality. In our time, historical reality is manifested in the fact that the revolution of rising expectations is erupting into social revolutions as a natural consequence of the suppression of these expectations by an assortment of *anciens régimes*. The United States, however, insists on interpreting these revolutions as instances of either centrally directed subversive plots or of military expansion of the great Communist powers. Consequently, the

United States has fallen victim to the most typical paranoid delusions—first a persecution mania and second a messianic mania, a conviction that the United States is destined to save the world from wickedness (Communism), even if it becomes necessary to destroy the world in the process.

The analogies between these aberrations and clinical manifestations of psychosis are striking enough. However, in attempting to trace the genesis of these societal psychoses, we must rely on pre-scientific speculation. It is not much consolation to note that psychiatry is virtually in a similar position. However, we have little choice in the matter if we wish to include the psychological approach in the study of total societies.

To the extent that societies are organized systems (and they give every indication that they are), they share common features with organisms, ecological systems, and machines. If we are reluctant to extend the notion of "psyche" to societies, this is, I suspect, only because we are at a loss to imagine how it "feels" to be a society. Our idea of "psyche" is still derived from introspection. But this is precisely how the idea of, say, a national psyche arises in the first place. It arises among men of imagination (philosophers of history, depth-psychologically oriented anthropologists, etc.) who have certain perceptions. We have no way at present of "checking out" their perceptions. We can only intuit their validity. For example, it seems to me that at the root of the Soviet psychosis of the thirties were the traumatic national experiences of Russia, going back to the days of the Tartar invasions. Russia had become fixated on personal autocracy as the only safeguard against fratricidal strife, which had surrendered the country to foreign domination in the thirteenth century and again in the seventeenth. I suspect that the Nazi psychosis was a reaction against the humiliation which the Germans felt had been imposed upon them by their cultural inferiors. I suspect that our own anti-Communist psychosis stems from the threat of the Communist ethos to the Puritan one, which still pervades the American national psyche. Such "insights" may be gratifying, but one cannot build a scientific theory on them. A scientific theory will have to deal not with "how it feels" but with *what happens*. How are historical events filtered and perverted to fit into established cognitive sets of the "national psyche"? How are decisions made? What restrictions are there on the available options *because* of the way the world is perceived by the decision makers? To what extent do decisions by the ruling elite actually guide or influence the "trajectory" of the system which is society?

These are the specific questions suggested by the psycho-organismic model of society, questions about social mechanisms which may add up to "sane" or "unsane" responses of a total society to its external and internal environments. Analogous questions on the level of an individual would be about the function or malfunction of neural mechanisms. One should think that it is easier to discover the social mechanisms, which determine the gross behavior patterns of societies, than to identify the intricate and vastly complex neural mechanisms, which determine the gross behavior of an individual. Social mechanisms can be observed in political organization, in economic pressures, in ways of reacting peculiar to different sectors of society, in the role of leadership, in the role of ideology and myth, etc. It would seem, then (somewhat paradoxically), that a "total society" might come to be understood in scientific terms sooner than the "whole organism," in spite of the fact that the methods of biological science are on the whole "harder" than those of social science. However, the study of social mechanisms and of cultural evolution is beset by difficulties of its own, which become especially severe when the "total society" succumbs to a fixed idea, be it the threat of "counter-revolution," of "racial debility," or of "communism," or of "hell fire." Here, then, is another analogy between societal and individual psychosis. Both make the victim blind to the compulsions which generate the psychosis. Both evoke destructive and self-destructive tendencies.

Our discussion of mathematical, evolutionary, and psychological approaches to the study of total societies has been conducted in three different languages. It is futile to ask which language should most appropriately encompass a "total" science of society. There is no unified language even in the physical sciences. For instance, the language of chemistry is different from that of physics; yet both sciences may be dealing with the same events. It is true that links have been established between physical and chemical concepts, and so our faith in the one-ness of the physical world is strengthened. Yet our minds cannot encompass this one-ness in its entirety, and we must pass from one set of concepts to another when we shift our focus of attention from one aspect of a phenomenon to another.

Similarly there is no question that the "total" society is far too complex to be encompassed by a single set of concepts. We shall be wise, therefore, to develop several paradigms at once in the hope that somewhere along the line, links can be established between conceptual systems and will reveal the underlying unity of the something we call "total society."

BIBLIOGRAPHY

Bertalanffy, Ludwig von. "General Systems Theory: a Critical Review," *General Systems*, 7, 1–22, 1962.

Boulding, Kenneth E. *The Image: Knowledge in Life and Society.* Ann Arbor: University of Michigan Press, pap., AA 47, 1956.

———. *The Meaning of the Twentieth Century.* New York: Harper, pap., CN 67, 1964.

Bronfenbrenner, Urie. "Allowing for Soviet Perceptions," in Roger Fisher, ed., *International Conflict and Behavioral Science.* New York: Basic Books, 1964.

Deutsch, Karl. *The Nerves of Government.* New York: Free Press of Glencoe, and London: Collier-Macmillan, 1963.

Emerson, A. E. "Ecology, Evolution, and Society," *American Naturalist*, 77, 77–118, 1943.

Erikson, Erik. *Childhood and Society.* New York: Norton, 1964.

Gerard, R. W. "Concepts and Principles of Biology," *Behavioral Science*, 3, 94–102, 1958.

Gerard, R. W., Kluckhohn, C., and Rapoport, A. "Biological and Cultural Evolution," *Behavioral Science*, 1, 6–14, 1956.

Gough, Kathleen. "The Crisis of the Nation-State," in Roger Fisher, ed., *International Conflict and Behavioral Science.* New York: Basic Books, 1964.

Korzybski, Alfred. *Manhood of Humanity.* New York: E. P. Dutton, 1921.

———. *Science and Sanity.* Lancaster, Pa.: Science Press, 1933.

Leites, N. C. *A Study of Bolshevism.* Glencoe, Ill.: Free Press, 1953.

———, and E. Bernaut. *Ritual of Liquidation.* Glencoe, Ill.: Free Press, 1954.

Mills, C. Wright. *The Causes of World War III*. New York: Simon and Schuster, 1958.

———. *The Power Elite*. New York: Oxford University Press, 1956.

Morgan, Lewis H. *Ancient Society*. Chicago: Charles H. Kerr, 1910.

Pringle, J. W. S. "On the Parallel Between Learning and Evolution," *General Systems*, 1, 90–110, 1956.

Rapoport, Anatol. *Fights, Games, and Debates*. Ann Arbor, Mich.: The University of Michigan Press, 1960.

———. *Strategy and Conscience*. New York: Harper & Row, 1964.

———. "Various Meanings of Theory," *American Political Science Review*, 12, 4, 972–88, 1958.

Richardson, Lewis F. *Arms and Insecurity*. Pittsburgh: The Boxwood Press, and Chicago: Quadrangle Press, 1960.

Wiener, Norbert. *The Human Use of Human Beings*. Garden City: Doubleday, 2nd ed. rev., Anchor A34, 1954.

———. *God and Golem, Inc.* Cambridge, Mass.: M.I.T. Press, 1964.

Wisdom, J. O. "The Hypothesis of Cybernetics," *General Systems*, 1, 111–22, 1956.

OPENING RESEARCH STRATEGIES

AMITAI ETZIONI and FREDRIC L. DUBOW[1]

SOME WORKPOINTS
FOR A MACROSOCIOLOGY

Although the relations among societal units have often been the focus of attention for political science, the distinctive characteristics of macroanalysis are seldom scrutinized by contemporary sociologists. In these few pages we can only suggest a few points which may be included in a theory of macroaction.[2] Before presenting a set of propositions regarding one macrosociological phenomenon, that of political unification, a few introductory remarks are called for. First, most of our analysis relates one macrovariable to another. Both the independent and dependent variables are attributes of societies, sub-societies, and supra-societal units. One can introduce into most of these propositions some data concerning the behavior of individuals or small groups such as those often employed by transactional, communications, or population models; but the main variables used here are macroscopic.

Second, we suggest that it is productive for macroscopic analysis to combine an analysis of systemic relations with an examination of power in the framework of a theory of action. Many systems theories, despite some recent modifications, neglect to include a conception of power. (The concept does not even appear in

[1] Fredric L. DuBow, of the University of California at Berkeley, prepared the final revision of this article. Ed.
[2] Additional elaborations will be presented in Amitai Etzioni, *The Active Society: A Macro-Theory of Societal and Political Processes* (New York: The Free Press, 1968).

the indices of the main theoretical works most often cited by sociologists.)[3] The concepts that are used characterize ongoing processes without depicting a guiding capacity. Concepts such as "élite," "leadership," and "decision making" rarely appear.

The general action schema posits an individual who chooses among means to fit his ends. When such schemas are projected onto the macro level, one finds an image of on-going interaction in which Negroes and whites, South and North, family and occupational groups are caught up in processes over which they have no control as collectivities. It is like the movement of cars without drivers. If this schema is to be applied to the study of societal processes such as economic development and political unification, we must return to questions of *action* on a macro level: who is "driving" these units, to what extent are the processes being controlled, and what differences do various attributes of the "drivers," as well as the cars, make for the routes followed?

THE ISLAND APPROACH

When we ask who guides a societal process, and who controls a societal unit, we realize that often units are treated as autonomous, as self-controlling. Before the limitations of this assumption can be pointed up, one conceptual distinction relevant at all levels of analysis, but particularly at the level of macroanalysis, needs to

[3] See, for instance, Talcott Parsons, *The Structure of Social Action* (Glencoe, Ill.: The Free Press, 1937); Parsons, *The Social System* (New York: The Free Press, 1951); Parsons and Edward A. Shils (eds.), *Toward a General Theory of Action* (New York: Harper Torchbooks, 1962).

be introduced; *a system's power space and action space are not necessarily coextensive* logically or empirically. Several significant consequences follow from this distinction.

The tendency to treat the social unit one studies as complete unto itself can be traced to anthropological methods where it might be justified for the study of isolated tribes. However, many organizational case studies proceed as if the corporation, the hospital, or the community under study were an island, a unit with no external bonds or limits, which interacts only with its "environment," but is not related to any other units. Some inputs come through the "gates" which the unit controls, but the unit is not conceived as having any *system* relationship with any other external unit.

An anthropological study of a factory demonstrates the kind of dimensions such research usually overlooks.[4] A strike in one division of the factory was suddenly followed by a strike in another. The anthropologist initially failed to explain why the second division, which had no operational relations with the first, would also strike. Then he realized that the factory was an integral part of the community in which workers in the first division tended to be sons of workers in the second. When the sons went on strike, the fathers felt that if they allowed their sons to gain a wage raise which they themselves did not receive, it would undermine the community's prestige structure. Thus, the linkage between the two divisions of the factors was found not in the factory but in the community. Thus, a unit assumed to be complete unto itself may often have significant linkages with other units.

[4] Conrad Arensberg, "Industry and the Community," *American Journal of Sociology*, Vol. 48 (1942).

One unit which is often depicted as an island is the national society. However, unlike change in the American society, few changes *in* other societies can be understood without accounting for the numerous and significant ways in which their parts are hooked into those of other societies. Consider, for example, the Dominican Republic under the Bosch government. If one were to assume that the Dominican Republic is a society unto itself, and were to examine the interaction between its various parts—perhaps seeking to determine the degree of stability of the Bosch government —one would soon realize that the Dominican Army had a close link with the U. S. Army, which provided it with arms, funds, and training, *and* that the Dominican government, whatever the legalities, did not control these inputs. Control is the key variable, for if the inputs were to come under the society's control mechanisms, they would be "digested" by the system and would be "consumed" in line with its structure.

Similarly, the Dominican Republic's economy was affected by the United States sugar quota. When Bosch came to power the country was in a deep depression, had little foreign currency, and about thirty per cent of the work force was unemployed.[5] A relatively small change in the sugar quota, i.e., the amount of sugar the Republic was allowed to export to the United States (above what it sells at world market prices), greatly affected the country's economic welfare.[6]

The importance of going beyond the "island" boundaries can be illustrated further in that conflicts and co-operations which at first seem internal are actually

[5] *New Republic*, March 2, 1963, p. 8.
[6] Abraham S. Lowenthal, "Foreign Aid as a Political Instrument," *Public Policy*, Vol. 14 (1965), p. 145.

in part the reflection of relationship between two or more external units which are linked with the internal ones. Thus as some disturbances among inmates in mental hospitals are explained by conflict among staff groups,[7] so part of what might at first seem as an internal Dominican societal conflict, is to be accounted for in terms of the relations between U.S. agencies, such as the Army, the Agency for International Development, congressional committees that deal with sugar quotas and other agencies.

Bolivia provides another example. Tin is Bolivia's biggest export, and consequently, one cannot understand any major Bolivian economic developments without considering the tin mines. Since nationalization of the tin mines following the 1952 Revolution, the output of the mines has declined due to the mining of low-grade veins, outmoded equipment, and the control of the labor force by left-oriented unions.[8] Between 1952 and 1962 the Bolivian government was slow to utilize the advice and financial aid of the United States, West Germany, and the Inter-American Development Bank to modernize the mines, because the miners objected to changes in work patterns, assignments, and pace which modernization entails. Part of the reluctance on the side of the government to act against the armed and organized miners was the relative weakness of the Bolivian Army. The Army was all but disbanded in 1952,[9] and its main force

[7] A. H. Stanton and M. S. Schwartz, *The Mental Hospital* (New York: Basic Books, 1954), especially pp. 342–65.

[8] J. David Bowen, "Bolivia's Revolution Comes of Age," *The Reporter*, September 26, 1963, pp. 34–36; and *The Economist*, 212, August 8, 1964, p. 544.

[9] Robert J. Alexander, "Bolivia," in Martin C. Needler (ed.), *Political Systems in Latin America* (Princeton: Van Nostrand, 1964), pp. 341–42.

consisted of sons of peasants. Under mounting Western pressure, the Bolivian government implemented parts of the Western-designed modernization scheme.

When in 1963–64 the showdown over the implementation of the modernization program between the civilian government and the unions seemed imminent, the army took over. Although the leftist miners are reported to have received some support from Castro's government, the U.S. assistance to the Bolivian Army was much greater, encompassing, and pervasive. While Castro's men were said to have "run" guns and distributed Marxist tracts in Spanish, the U.S. provided tanks, airplanes, modern communications systems, and massive small-arms training and funds.[10] The newly strengthened Bolivian army neutralized the unions, but also unseated the government and de-emphasized much of its development-oriented programs.

This change of fortune *in* the Bolivian society, from a stalemate between a civilian elected government and the left-leaning labor unions to a military junta, may at first seem owing to some internal Bolivian developments. Actually *one* of the most important developments was a ten-year U.S. strengthening of the Bolivian Army. Of course, other factors were at work. There is no lack of precedents of military coups in Latin America, and the Bolivian tradition of democracy was both young and not without flaws. It should be noted, however, that (a) in Bolivia, as in Mexico, but unlike most other Latin American countries, the

[10] This statement is based on interviews by A. Etzioni with the U.S. ambassador to Bolivia, the chief of the U.S. Army Mission in Bolivia, and with two Bolivian army officers during a field trip in 1964. See also The New York *Times,* July 6, 1966, editorial page.

army had been disbanded, its social base, the aristoc-
racy, eroded, and the new army initiated as a "popular" force; (b) that precisely because of the weakness of the other societal institutions, the heavy
concentration of U.S. support in one sector, the military, seemed to have had a tipping effect.

One could cite many other examples, but only the
details would be different.[11] These examples suggest
that the island approach is not valid; it is a mistake to
treat countries as autonomous systems, meaning by
systems that when a factor outside the system works
on one of the members, changes in its behavior are
explainable primarily in terms of its relations to other
members and changes in them. If one wishes to do a
*satisfactory systems analysis, it will be necessary to
look beyond the boundaries of a particular society to
the ties which link it to other societies.* It does not have
to be the United States or a former colonial power. If
one studies Uruguay, it may be critical to consider
Argentina and Brazil.[12] Analysis of social change in
Trinidad may involve British Guiana. The degree of
economic and defense co-operation between Denmark, Norway, and Sweden correlates highly with the
state of affairs between the three great powers to
which these Scandinavian countries relate. The trade

[11] Some of the literature on Turkey demonstrates the same
point in a different part of the world. Frederick Frey has analyzed political change in Turkey with little reference to external
factors in *The Turkish Political Elite* (Cambridge, Mass.: Massachusetts Institute of Technology Press, 1965). D. Rustow
points to the role of U.S. military aid in Robert E. Ward and
Dankwart A. Rustow, *Political Development in Turkey and
Japan* (Princeton: Princeton University Press, 1964), pp. 352–
88.

[12] Russell H. Fitzgibbon, *Uruguay: Portrait of a Democracy*
(New Brunswick, N.J.: Rutgers University Press, 1954), esp.
pp. 3–43.

of Scandinavian countries with each other was approximately 12 per cent of their total foreign trade. But when Germany, the Soviet Union, and Great Britain were in conflict, as in World War I, the amount of trade among the Scandinavian countries increased to approximately 30 per cent, only to return to 12 per cent after peace was restored.[13]

One misunderstanding is to be avoided: we do not imply that a big power can dictate or direct the social change of a small country. In fact, the data indicate clearly that outside powers cannot guide change even for the smallest country. The smaller West Indian islands, for example, are very weak by any definition; hundreds of American corporations have much larger incomes and assets than these islands. Even so, Great Britain could not even make them stay in the Federation of the West Indies if they did not wish it.[14] But while an outside power cannot direct a small country's social change, it can interfere in it to such a magnitude that, to understand the process, one must trace the links—institutionalized ties and power hierarchies, not simply transactional flows or exchange—between the small country's sectors and outside sectors.[15]

[13] Eli F. Heckscher, Kurt Bergendahl, Wilhelm Keilhan, Einar Cohn, and Thorstein Thorsteinsson, *Sweden, Norway, Denmark and Iceland in the World War* (New Haven: Yale University Press, 1930), pp. 101–3; and Frantz Wendt, *The Nordic Council and Cooperation in Scandinavia* (Copenhagen: Hunksgaard, 1959), p. 28.

[14] See Amitai Etzioni, *Political Unification* (New York: Holt, Rinehart and Winston, 1965), pp. 138–83.

[15] For a good example of a "non-island" approach to African affairs, see Immanuel Wallerstein, "African Unity Reassessed," *Africa Report*, 11 (April 1966), p. 41–46.

UNIFICATION: AN INTERSOCIETAL PROCESS

When a specific process of societal change is studied —in this case, *political unification* will serve as one example of such a process—three questions must be asked. First, who is controlling the process (in terms of who is giving political guidance)? In the case of the West Indian Federation, Great Britain played a significant role. This does not mean that the West Indian islands had no effect on the process, but that an important part of the story will have to be told in terms of an external élite which has a significant degree of control over the process.

Second, how well does the given external guidance "fit" the relationships *in* the system which is being guided? Since no outside power has yet developed a perfect model for intervention, *external élite guidance often conflicts with the existing power structure of the system on which it imposes itself*. One may ask about an external power projection into a system; what does it emphasize and what does it de-emphasize? In the West Indies, Jamaica and Trinidad are much more powerful than the other eight small islands. They have 80 per cent of the GNP; Jamaica found aluminum, while Trinidad found oil.[16] Not every asset leads inexorably to power. A country can have oil and not be powerful, but in the case of Jamaica and Trinidad, assets and power did associate: two better-off islands were powerful; each of the eight

[16] H. W. Springer, "The West Indies Emergent: Problems and Prospects," in David Lowenthal (ed.), *The West Indies Federation: Perspectives on a New Nation*, American Geographical Society Research Series, No. 23 (New York: Columbia University Press, 1961), p. 8.

small islands was weak. Many of the differences go above and beyond territory and population. The two powerful islands have industry, the small islands are agricultural; Jamaica and Trinidad are developing, the small islands are stagnant.[17]

Great Britain, in its projection into the situation, favored the small islands. One reason is that they are more pro-British than Jamaica and Trinidad. Another reason is that Britain has long felt a close affinity to Barbados, one of the small islands. Britain suggested a constitution which gave a majority in the House of Representatives to the small islands, even though more than 80 per cent of the population is on Jamaica and Trinidad. The small islands had even a larger majority in the Senate, where voting was conducted by territories. The small islands used these majorities to pass a progressive federal income tax, which meant that Jamaica and Trinidad would have to pay much more than the small islands because their income per capita is about twice that of the others.

All this suggests that the "fit" between the external élite's projected institutional structure and the power relation among the West Indian participants was a poor one. As a consequence, there was a clash between the system's power distribution and the institutional patterns. Theoretically, if the external intervention is massive enough, a system's internal power nexus could be redistributed to fit the institutional structure projected on to it. If Britain, for example, had been willing to pay the price of making the small islands as rich as Jamaica and Trinidad, the real power distribution

---

[17] An examination of changes in income distribution by per cent of the GNP during the fifties clearly illustrates this trend. See *National Income Statistics, The West Indies* (Trinidad: Federal Statistical Office, 1960), p. 21; and Lowenthal, *op. cit.*, p. 99.

might have been brought into line with the one Britain favored. But Britain was not willing, and probably not able, to finance such a change; as a consequence, the institutional structure collapsed. The larger islands seceded and the Federation was dismantled.

The third question concerns "internalization," a term borrowed from psychology for purposes of analogy. In the process of unifying a system, i.e., increase in its level of integration, internalization of power often takes place. That is, at point two in time as compared with point one, the unification process is more controlled by member élites than by non-member (i.e., external) ones. The changing U.S. relationship with Europe is an example. In 1945, each of the six European Economic Community countries was directly linked to the U.S., which had a measure of influence not just on their internal changes but also on their relations to each other (e.g., the U.S. encouraged unification). Over the years, especially since the late fifties, much of this influence has passed to internal élites—in part to De Gaulle's France, in part to the EEC Executive Commission. Such internalization often involves a struggle between the internal and external élites, and the outcome of this struggle, the form it takes, determines, to a considerable degree, both the structure of the system which is internalizing the control and the system's relationship with the external élite.

These are just a few brief illustrations of a macroanalysis of action, which includes a power analysis and which avoids the island approach. What follows is a set of seventeen propositions that seem useful in exploring the problems of initiating and propagating bonds among units that previously have been unrelated or less related. We proceed by presenting a set of propositions rather than more illustrative material.

Although each case of an attempted unification, or any other social process, is unique in that any particular set of factors is unlikely to appear in the same form, by studying those factors which reappear in different combinations and in different contexts, one can expect to gain some insights into the dynamics of a particular unification from an analytic study of others. The propositions present a set of uniformities which have been developed from a study of four attempts at inter-societal unification.[18] The applicability of these propositions to a wider range of cases remains an open but, we believe, fruitful question.

INTEGRATING POWER: EFFECTIVE DISTRIBUTION

Degree of Élitism

1. Unions that have fewer élite-units will tend to be more successful than unions that have more. In particular, unions having one élite will be more successful than those having two, and those with two more than those with three.

2. Egalitarian unions, whether they develop system-élites or not, tend to be similar in their degree of success to mono-élite unions.

3. Egalitarian unions tend to be less decisive than élitist unions, but more capable in generating commitments.

The Internalization of Élites

4. The external élite tends to enhance the success of unification the more the direction of its application

[18] Some empirical evidence in support of these propositions, based on the study of four cases, is presented in Amitai Etzioni, *Political Unification, op. cit.*

of power coincides with the power structure of the emerging union, and to hinder it the more the application of this power is counter to the emerging structure.

5. As the level of integration and the scope of a union increase, the union tends to internalize the functions performed, as well as the authority held and the loyalties commanded by the external élite.

INTEGRATING POWER: EFFECTIVE COMPOSITION

Differences in Kind of Power

6. The more identitive power the élite initiating, and guiding unification command or the union-system builds up, the more successful unification tends to be.

7. The more utilitarian power the élites initiating and guiding unification command or the union-system builds up, the more successful unification tends to be.

8. The relation between the application of coercive power and the success of unification is curvilinear. (That is, in contrast to the two other kinds of power, the higher application of force, above a given level, is expected to produce less, not more, unification, all other things being equal.)

Differences in Communication and Responsiveness

9. A union is more successful the more effective its upward and downward *communication* channels are and the more *responsive* its power élites are to the communication received.

10. The stability of a union is undermined and its growth curtailed when the avenues of *political representation* are clogged or closed. (Note: political representation is viewed as a central avenue of power-backed communication.)

11. *Secession* of alienated units will be much more common than revolution in unions as compared to political communities.

12. The ratio will change in favor of revolutions as the process of unification increases the level of integration and scope of the unions.

INTEGRATING POWER: A DYNAMIC PERSPECTIVE

Unit-Preparation and Power Requirements

13. The amount of power needed to *increase* the level of integration and to extend the scope of a union tends to be higher than that needed to *maintain* a given level of integration and scope.

Mature Unions

14. Integrating power needed tends to be greater to maintain a *premature* unification effort than a *mature* one; and even smaller, at least in the initial stage, to maintain an *overdue* one.

15. *Acceleration* strategy tends to be more successful in the mature and overdue unions and *deceleration* strategy in the premature unions.

Subunits and Unification

16. For the initial stages of unification, *building up* the union, *rather than reallocation* among units or subunits, tends to be more effective.

17. The *coercive showdown* of a union tends to come at a particular point in its life history: (a) as the power of external élites declines, (b) before the union's utilitarian and identitive systems and power are built up, or (c) after they have weakened.

Political unification is just one societal process in which questions of guidance and of macroscopic emergent properties form an essential part of the analysis. Eventually, we suggest, propositions can be developed to describe other societal processes as well as macroaction in general.

MARION J. LEVY, JR.

FAMILY STRUCTURE AND THE HOLISTIC ANALYSIS OF SOCIETIES[1]

Although one has to make an attempt at holistic analysis to get anywhere with any science, I think that in the field of sociology virtually no one has tried it explicitly nor, indeed, is interested in it. Despite ideological traditions suggesting concern with generalizations about any society, nearly all the work in this field is about isolated aspects of a single type of society. Of course, implicitly or explicitly, one has to state something about the system concerned and about its interdependent parts. This, however, does not mean that the focus of interest is "the real thing." Here again, we in the social sciences, with the possible exception of economics, have been so preoccupied with being right (perhaps this is a function of the search for findings with known "important" applications) that we have lost sight of what science is all about. I take it that we would generally agree that —while one may have great faith that scientific findings sooner or later turn out to have applications— nevertheless, the scientific game, as played in the more highly developed instances, is a search for highly generalized sets of theories, preferably in terms of as small a number of variables as possible (as long as

[1] This material is an adaptation of that by the author which appears in A. J. Coale *et al.* (eds.), *Aspects of the Analysis of Family Structure* (Princeton, N.J.: Princeton University Press, 1965), pp. 1–63.

the number of variables is greater than one, so that they are not monistic statements). The scientific concern is not so much with being right as with being fruitful for the further development of such propositions. The end of the game is propositions which are conceivably falsifiable and preferably informative, regardless of whether they are temporarily confirmed *or* falsified. I wish to discuss this kind of activity in terms of some of my current work.

What can one say about *any* society? One first must define the unit of analysis, and then suggest some subcategories of this unit that are interdependent and will apply in any time and place. Because organizational subsystems and the functions of operating in terms of these are so variable, it is difficult to specify the *concrete* structural requisites of any and all societies—the organizational requisites of any and all societies. For that reason I have tried to develop the *analytic* structural requisites of any society,[2] for, in those terms, it is possible to generalize. I argued then that some sort of family organization was universally present in any society, but that I could not demonstrate that it was a concrete structural requisite of any and all societies. I have in recent years returned to this issue because other work has provided a lead I did not have at that time. It now seems that the family *is* a concrete structural requisite of any and all societies, and hence some sort of interrelating organization is also a concrete structural requisite. Most analyses of societies that attempt a holistic picture—generally anthropological studies—describe the geographical setting and the provenance of the society, and then proceed to discuss its kinship system without any

[2] Marion J. Levy, Jr., *The Structure of Society* (Princeton, N.J.: Princeton University Press, 1952).

theoretical justification for doing so. I believe that approach is sound because family structure provides the most general lead into any society.

I would define *kinship structure* as any membership unit, i.e., any organization, whose members are chosen (or "selected," or "become members," or are "deemed members") as a function of orientations, at least in part, to considerations of biological descent and/or regularized sexual intercourse of some sort. This definition generates a set of four possible types of concrete structures. The first are non-kinship structures—organizations whose members are not oriented even in part to biological descent (real or assumed) or to sexual intercourse. That leaves three kinds of kinship structure. First are those oriented at least in part to sexual intercourse, but not to descent. (This would include dyadic relationships between customer and prostitute, or more complicated membership units of this sort. I would consider this kinship if only because of the implications it has for other types of organizations, and the possibility of getting further involved through such things as pregnancy.)

The other two kinship structures are (a) those oriented at least in part to descent, but not to sexual intercourse as such (some, if not all clans would be organizations of this sort), and (b) the family, which, by definition, is oriented at least in part to both these considerations.

Another distinction is that between ideal and actual structures. Ideal structure may be defined as any pattern or uniformity of action to which people feel they should adhere. For example, it is an ideal structure of American society that bullying is a bad thing. An extraordinary number of Americans would tell you so and it is probable that, on some level, they "mean" this. Actual structures are those patterns in terms of which the individuals *in fact* behave (from the point of view of a theoretically omniscient observer).

Using the ideal/actual distinction, several generalizations will apply universally. There are no people who are unaware of the distinction between the way in which they do behave (or their colleagues behave) and the way they would prefer to have behavior take place. These two sets of structures never coincide perfectly for any given social system as a whole. There are always some discrepancies between what people say they would like to do (or should do or ought to do) and the way in which they in fact behave. Nowhere, and at no time, are people completely unaware of such discrepancies, although they may not be aware of all of them. Some of the sources of stress and strain characteristic of any social system inhere in (or result from, or are a function of) the fact that the ideal and actual structures do not coincide. Not only are people aware of such discrepancies, but they are to some extent also upset by them. Not paradoxically, however, to some extent the possibilities of integration of a particular system inhere in the fact that ideal and actual structures do not coincide. For example, the Chinese in the Imperial period had as one ideal structure a large number of sons per family unit. They also had as an ideal structure equal inheritance among sons, a vital factor in the history of China. Contrary to many analyses, Chinese society has not been a feudal society in any precise sense for well over two thousand years, partly because of this concept of equal inheritance among sons. Even, however, in a situation in which only slightly more than two children per marital pair survived to maturity, land was subdivided to the point of marginal subsistence (the probability there being that 25 per cent of these pairs would include two males, 25 per cent two females, and 50 per cent one male and one female, who would eventually intermarry). Had the Chinese achieved their ideal structure with regard to family size, the tradition of equal inheritance could not have been maintained.

The failure of ideal and actual structures to coincide cannot be explained solely in terms of hypocrisy. Two other relevant generalizations are more problematical. One is that ideal and actual structures cannot coincide perfectly because that would tax the cognitive capacities of individuals. It would require that everyone know perfectly all structures, know perfectly how to adjust to them, and be aware of all needs for adjustments. This is, of course, highly unlikely and historically unprecedented. The second generalization is that if ideal/actual correspondence were achieved, the resulting system would be perfectly brittle. Any change in the setting of such a system, with implications for interdependency of that and other systems, would require a complete, instantaneous renovation of the system to maintain the relationship between ideal and actual structures.

I should like to distinguish between *basic* and *intermediate*. By "basic," I mean those structures, bits of knowledge or whatever, that every member of the system is expected to acquire at some point in the life cycle or during his membership in the organization concerned. By "intermediate," I mean those structures that only some proportion or segment of that population are expected to acquire. (Incidentally, probably one of the most highly general forms of intermediate role differentiation is sex role differentiation.) One may distinguish two types of *have-nots*. There are what might be termed *normal have-nots*. If literacy is part of the basic cognition of the society, two-year-olds, who are ordinarily illiterate, can be called normal have-nots with regard to the basic cognition of literacy. There are, in addition, the *pathological have-nots*. They may be physiologically pathological—brain-damaged children, in this case—or they may be in some sense socially pathological.

Finally, I distinguish between relatively modernized societies and relatively nonmodernized ones, by examples. Societies like the United States, West Germany, France, Japan and the Soviet Union are relatively or highly modernized. The Chinese, the Indians, the Vietnamese, most of Latin America (certainly outside the major urban centers) are relatively nonmodernized.

To return to the subject of the family, everything that has ever been identified as a society has developed some form of family structure. In all known societies the family has some universally common characteristics, e.g., an incest taboo, as an ideal structure. As a minimum, the incest taboo always covers the relationships between father/daughter, mother/son and sister/brother. Most accepted violations occur among a particular subset of individuals, such as a Pharaonic family—never for the membership as a whole. Further, the variations themselves, as far as these ideals are concerned, are highly structured. Apparently, father/daughter incest is considerably more frequent than the others, the brother/sister permutation presumably being next most common.

There are certain biological bases for maintaining that the family is a requisite. Social scientists have for so long objected to the biological determinism of Watsonian psychology, that they are still in the throes of implying something equally fallacious, i.e., that biology has nothing to do with the case. The question is how to strike an accurate balance. Some maintain, for example, that there are good biological reasons for the fondling of neonates by biological mothers. And there certainly are biological explanations of the fact that the infant will respond to such attention and reinforce the relationship. This is not to say that these operations cannot be offset, that there are not mothers who will reject their children. But if it is true that fondling and response are factors in establishing interpersonal solidarity, regular affective relations with the mother, it is easy to build up some sort of kinship or family unit on that basis.

There are psychological bases for considering this structure of solidarity necessary to the organization and the society in general. One such psychological basis is the effect on mothers of the deprivation of opportunities for child care. It is not a matter of chance, and not just a matter of social conditioning, that mothers deprived at birth of neonates have problems of adjustment. Indeed, this would be expected in view of the magnitude of the hormonal changes characteristic of the birth process and pregnancy. To deprive mothers of their infants would result not only in certain problems with the infants, sooner or later, but also great problems with the mothers.

The effect of this type of deprivation on children is a cliché of our time. Infants must have a certain amount of close affective response and attention if they are to develop into what we call human beings, if they are to be socializable. There are alternatives to the actual participation of the biological mother in this process, but I suspect that the number of infants to whom a given individual can minister at any given point in time (unless he or she is a virtuoso of this sort of affective attention) is that roughly consistent with maximum fertility rates. If nurses could not be trained to attend to more infants than the biological mothers could handle, general infant-rearing by nurses would simply be a complicated game of musical chairs.

There are also social bases for the argument that a family is a requisite. There is no functional equivalent to a family; there is no organization in terms of which the same set of requisite performances has taken place or is likely to take place in terms of any society. For one thing, virtually all individuals in all known societies in history have acquired substantial proportions of their basic learning in a family context. Despite much concern that the family is losing its function in relatively modernized societies, almost all individuals still learn to walk, to talk, to eat, to move their bowels, to receive and give affection, and to understand allocation of power and responsibility, in a family context. The behavior of the vast majority of individuals throughout history, i.e., virtually all members of all relatively non-modernized societies, has *in fact* been family-oriented. This obtains even if some other organizational foci take precedence over the family. For example, Japanese in the Tokugawa period sacrificed their families quite willingly to the interests of their lord if they were given the opportunity, but rarely did they have an opportunity to do so, and by far the most of what they did was carried out in terms of family-oriented organizational foci. This primarily means that, during the life cycle, all learning, all cognition—basic and intermediate—was acquired in a family context. One of the really revolutionary things about the process of modernization is that, for the first time, many acquire learning outside a family structure. Furthermore, the family is always the context in

which control is initially learned. Any subsequent
learning about allocation of power and responsibility
is ordinarily superimposed on family responses to this
condition. Even if it were possible to obtain complete
permissiveness with regard to infants, which it is not,
that in itself would be a structure of allocation of
power and responsibility. For all relatively nonmodernized societies, family control is *the* main basis for
decentralized control. While it is interesting to
contemplate theories of total despotism, no relatively
nonmodernized society has ever been stable over long
periods of time if it was overwhelmingly centralized.
All of the stable societies represent combinations of
centralization and decentralization.

Corresponding propositions can be made for the
centrality of the family in economic allocation. For all
relatively nonmodernized societies, the family is the
main economic unit for the vast majority of people.
The same thing can be maintained also for emotional
life, learning to give and receive affection, or not.
Finally, the family is always the major focus of relief
organizations, at least outside of relatively modernized contexts.

The family has a peculiar relationship to the life
cycle of the individual: if one differentiates age roles
on the basis of absolute age—infancy, childhood,
adulthood, and old age—a family is the only organization in terms of which the individuals of virtually all
known societies ordinarily *always* have some sort of
age role throughout the life cycle.

Finally, all organizations other than families can be
divided into two categories with respect to the articulation of family and nonfamily organizational contexts.
There are those organizations in terms of which,
ideally speaking, family considerations are supposed

to influence the behavior of the individual. This is characteristic of most organizations in relatively non-modernized societies. However, in relatively modernized ones, there is characteristically a great proliferation of organizations in terms of which, ideally speaking, what happens in the family context is *not* supposed to influence behavior. But, of course, it does. The family is the only organizational context for all societies in terms of which the individual always has one or more roles that ideally and/or actually affect his behavior in terms of every other organization. For that reason alone, the family is the most general structural lead-in for the structural analysis of any society, including highly modernized societies.

Nepotism is a universal problem. The ways in which it is handled vary, as do the attitudes towards it, but it is always present in some respect. Therefore, I would maintain not only that the family as an organization is a requisite of any society, but that it is also the most relevant structure for all others in all societies. There are more lead-ins from the family than there are from any other single structure for all societies.

It is interesting to examine the actual trans-societal convergence of family structures, despite the existence of great variations in ideal structures. The actual closure of ideal and actual structures is considerable. For example, in descriptions of various societies, it is frequently alleged that they are polygynous or polyandrous. The implication is that most, if not all male members of the polygynous society have two or more wives after reaching maturity. Such a statement is clearly false and can be shown to be so. The ratio of males to females at birth is of the order of 102:100, varying to as much as 107:100. Males are considerably less viable than females even after birth, so that as they approach marital ages the ratio is closer to one. *In utero*, the male/female ratio may very well be of the order of 140:100 to 150:100.[3]

This is a clear-cut case in which attention to the distinction between ideal and actual structures is important. Whenever someone describes a society as polygynous, what it really implies is that polygyny is an ideal structure, that a small minority of members of the society achieve it, and that that minority is almost certainly an élite, by virtue of the fact that they *do* achieve it.[4]

I would suggest a strategy of analysis involving demography. Family organizations can proliferate in terms of demographic factors along two axes: vertically in terms of numbers of generations represented, and horizontally in terms of marital spouse pairs of

[3] This statement *like* others throughout should be regarded as an hypothesis about the facts. It rests on hearsay evidence from demographers, who speculate that early miscarriages are more likely to be of male than female fetuses.

The second most revolutionary practical social possibility I have ever heard, was suggested recently by a medical person who felt medical researchers were on the threshold of reducing radically the male mortality *in utero*. If so, when the ratio of males to females at age eighteen approaches 140:100, we will witness unprecedented revolution.

The most radical proposal, ideological possibilities to the contrary notwithstanding, has to do with the successful separation of male sperm into those determining male as opposed to female offspring. This plus "the pill" and various intrauterine devices will make determinations of the sex of offspring feasible at the time of conception for the first time in history. Now, the vast majority of all males express a preference for male offspring and so do the vast majority of all females. Given the possibility of accurate, cheap, safe pre-selection, these ratios might easily reach as high as 10:1, with obvious results.

[4] Ansley J. Coale has demonstrated to me that it is possible to have plural wives for the vast majority of males if, for example, all males wait until age thirty to marry and all females marry at age twenty. Such gaps are not usual in descriptions of societies held to be polygynous.

either sons or daughters of a given generation. The largest possible ideal of this sort the world has ever known, historically, is the extended family (F_e)[5] of traditional Chinese society, for which the ideal was to combine the members of as many generations as possible, and all of the sons and all of their unmarried daughters of any given generation for as long as possible. Intermediate to this is the stem family (F_s) in which, as in the case of Japan, the eldest son usually remained a member of the family unit and younger sons married to start independent families. Finally, there is the nuclear family (F_n). Here, I would take issue with Parsons, Murdock, and others. The nuclear family is not the *ideal* structure of every society. The *reductio ad absurdum* with regard to that particular proposition is trivially easy. Take this example, which assumes that the nuclear family is regarded as the ideal of any society in some sense: there is a grandmother living with her son, his wife and their son. If there is a sexual relationship between the grandmother and the grandson, it is *interfamily* incest; if there is a sexual relationship between mother and son, it is *intrafamily* incest. Apparently, no society makes such a distinction. If a man with two wives has a son by one and a daughter by the other, then while both wives live, a sexual relationship between the daughter's mother and the husband's son is interfamily incest. If one of the wives dies, leaving the other to become sole mother, it becomes intrafamily incest—as would brother-sister incest in a similar situation. To distinguish marital pairs and their children does not mean that the nuclear family is a unit of solidarity for the members of that society, unless it is made true

[5] This and subsequent symbols are here introduced for the sake of later brevity.

by definition. Murdock and Parsons define "the family"
as consisting of father, mother, and non-adult children.
Thus their concept of the nuclear family is true, but
it is also meaningless.

Dividing all societies in world history into, first, societies without any modern medical technology (S_1),
societies with modern medical technology plus high
levels of modernization in general (S_{2a}), and those
societies whose members have imported modern
medical technology, but not the other structures of
modernization (S_{2b}), very curious things follow. It
makes much less difference than one might think
whether F_e, F_s, or F_n is an ideal structure of societies
of the type of S_1. It can be shown that the vast majority of these societies have a birth/death ratio of the
order of 50:50. With markedly higher birth rates, they
long since would have overpopulated the earth. With
markedly lower birth rates, they would have quickly
become extinct and, in the process, would have supported the hypotheses in question even more radically.
If F_n and S_1 are associated, it can be shown that for
the F_n's the average number of members is 4+, which
I would assign an index number of 1. Under the same
conditions, the index number for F_e is only 1.75, or an
average of 7 members for each extended family. Re-
laxing an extreme adoption assumption, the index for
F_e drops immediately to 1.36. Moving to F_s, the index
number is only 1.16.

The reasoning behind this is perfectly simple: very
few grandparents long survive the birth of their first
grandchild, and very few more than two siblings per
generation survive to maturity in the context of societies of the type S_1. Thus, there is little difference in
the curves of distribution of numbers of members in
the various ideal family structures. From this, one may

argue that well over 50 per cent—probably upward of 80 per cent—of all individuals in history who have lived in terms of societies without modern technology, have *in fact* lived in terms of families in which the number of members was the same as it would have been had their ideal been the nuclear family. That is the significant aspect of what Parsons and Murdock were talking about.[6]

Convergence between ideal and actual structures using other demographic measures—numbers of generations represented, number of spouse pairs—will all be less than the 75 per cent obtained using numbers of individuals as the measure. They all involve at least one individual, and only if all of the variance inhered, for example, in generational representatives, could this be as much as the 75 per cent variation.

Carl Helm, P. Demeny, F. F. Stephan, C. F. Westhoff, and I are now attempting to apply these and other insights to the problem of family composition under varying socio-economic conditions. We are engaged in running a computer program designed to calculate the distributions of marital spouse pairs, etc., for any combination of ideal family structures, given any set of mortality/fertility statistics. If we are correct, then, that the divergence of the actual from the ideal nuclear structure is a maximum of 75 per cent with regard to numbers of individuals, and considerably less with regard to other factors, it would be

---

[6] For societies of type S_{2a}, virtually 100 per cent of the members hold ideal structures of F_n so that there will be no divergence there. Indices for S_{2b} societies can increase radically but can be shown to be unstable. Therefore, regardless of variations in ideal structures, well over 50 per cent, and maybe upward of 80 per cent of all people live or have lived in the same types of families—as far as number of members is concerned—as they would have done if F_n had been the ideal structure.

fruitful to set up façade hypotheses in demographic terms. As a strategy of analysis, it would seem sensible to ask what the implications of other questions about family structure would be for demographic factors. If the computer analysis I mentioned above is successful, it will be possible to generalize the findings and derive predictions of some accuracy for any set or subset of ideal structures. It would also be possible to predict with accuracy the other factors in question. For example, if it is maintained, as it was at one time, that birth order has something to do with personality characteristics, it ought to be possible to predict, given any particular ideal structure, the incidence of certain personality characteristics in that society. Further, it should be possible to verify the tenability of such propositions in terms of, first, the possibility of such individuals being present, and, second, the identification of them.

This, it seems to me, provides a quite general lead-in to the analysis of the structure of any society in terms of a small number of variables. The number of variables can be reduced by dropping the S_1/S_2 distinction and performing the analysis with the aid of demographic tables encompassing all possibilities, since some reasonable parameters are not difficult to fix. There are, after all, limits to the number of births possible for any given set of women, and short of solving the problem of mortality, there are limits to the decline of deaths.

ABRAM KARDINER

MODELS FOR THE STUDY OF COLLAPSE OF SOCIAL HOMEOSTASIS IN A SOCIETY

Psychoanalysis is a holistic psychology that deals with molar units of human adaptation, is able to identify the approximate origins of these molar units, and to differentiate between effective and ineffectual adaptive patterns. This psychology is therefore able to appraise the response of the individual organism to the external conditions furnished by the natural, human, and intraorganismic environments.

The ability of this psychology to say something about social homeostasis is based on its capacity to evaluate the impact of institutions on man. Society, not being an organism, has no built-in homeostats. These must be built into the individual organism. In the twenties the anthropologists were teaching that some people do one thing and some do another. The implication was that all institutional arrangements were viable and could be accepted by the individual without detriment to his personal adaptation or to the adaptation of his society. This has proved to be untrue.

It is of special interest to study societies that are functioning effectively, but which are undergoing subtle changes that will destroy the homeostatic balance. Such change is called revolutionary. The great dread of humanity today is that once the homeostasis collapses there is unleashed a social chaos that takes on a destructive character. This destructiveness must be shunted, satisfied, or be subjected to enforced homeostasis, the future of which is not likely to be very stable.

I want therefore to discuss two types of homeostatic collapse: one is not revolutionary, the other is. The first is the abrupt change in social patterning in Tanala. The other is the American Negro revolution.

The best example I know of the phenomenology of social change is furnished by Linton's account of the consequences of the change from the dry to the wet method of rice cultivation in a tribe in Madagascar.[1] To understand the manifestations of this concealed revolution, it is essential to discuss the social patterning during the dry-cultivation period and make some conjectures about the kind of personality engendered by this social patterning.

The group we are studying lived in mountainous country well suited for the cutting and burning method of rice culture. The soil was poor and required fifteen years of fallowing. The rice crop was stored by the family and prorated to the family members as needed. They had no magic rituals about rice production, i.e., it had no problems that could not be solved by themselves, but there were some rituals to protect crops against hail and locusts. They had cattle but did not use them for food.

The social organization consisted of a village held by a *gens.* The available land was divided into wards, each of which was owned by a lineage which worked its section independently of the other *gentes.* Each year the entire group moved to a new area. The social organization was communal as far as food production was concerned. Everything else was individually

[1] For a fuller discussion, see Abram Kardiner, *The Individual and His Society* (New York: Columbia University Press, 1939).

owned. Money and cattle had no relation to the subsistence economy, but did have prestige value. Money
was the only form of property subject to theft and was
therefore carefully concealed. Apart from the value of
money for land purchase, and hence for setting up a
new lineage, there was no difference in living standards between rich and poor. The only way to become
wealthy was to raise cattle or to become a medicine
man (*ombiasy*).

Power to make decisions was vested largely in the
family or lineage head. Since there was so little opportunity for initiative, ingratiation with the father
was the chief means for insuring security. This was not
true for the oldest son, who was immune from labor
and would succeed to the family headship.

The village was therefore a kind of extended family
consisting of the headman (and wives) and sons (and
wives). Control of lineage passed from headman to
oldest son. The headman organized work, divided land
for cultivation, took charge of funerals and settled dis-
putes among lineage members. He had a direct claim
on the labor of all males. The headman was a kind of
king or dictator.

Only a few details about the individual life cycle are
important to us. The mother carried the child on a belt
pad. They had no swaddling material—or claim not
to have had any. As a consequence, the mother was
constantly being soiled by the child. This acts as an in-
centive to premature induction into sphincter control,
which was begun at two months and generally com-
pleted at six months. It was done by beating the child
mercilessly until somehow it got the idea that relaxa-
tion of sphincters leads to pain. The child therefore
learned obedience at a very early age and learned to
respect power. Ingratiation or compliance was learned

as the safest form of adaptation. Hence not much discipline was required during growth.

The main rivalries in the society were between brothers. Blood brotherhood-bond is a way of controlling the mutual hostility. It should be mentioned here that none of the other institutions in this society were very different from those of other patriarchal societies. But there was one outstanding feature. A good deal more homosexuality and transvestitism occurred in this society than in most. We shall later discuss the reasons for this. (Transvestites are not necessarily homosexual. It is the common refuge for the impotent man.) Homosexuals and transvestites were recruited from among younger sons.

These are the essentials of the dry rice culture and the social organization necessary to carry it out. The wet rice culture was copied from their neighbors to the east—the Betsileo. This method had existed for a long time alongside the dry rice method. The new method of wet rice culture broke up the old social organization and made necessary a new style of social patterning. Members of the old culture were unable to cope with these new patterns.

The old social organization was not capriciously or arbitrarily set up. It was suited to a semi-nomadic culture whose efficiency was maintained by obligatory co-operation in a hierarchy of rank. Submissiveness and ingratiation were adequate adaptive attitudes which for many generations had kept the social organization effective.

Adaptation under the new conditions for wet rice required a different order of social patterning, and the new patterning required a personality development different from the old. In the new society submissiveness and ingratiation did no good. Aggressiveness and pugnacity were required. It was a society which the strong would ultimately control.

Since the new cultivation was in swamps, which were permanent sites, the nomadic pattern of the society ceased. The land could not be exhausted. The old communal organization broke up; the large *gentes* disintegrated and the private entrepreneur had to move wherever there were swamps. Individual enterprise was born.

The old mobile villages were self-contained and endogamous. The settled villages were much less so. The members of the old *gens* were now separated by wide distances, and family members could be called together on ceremonial occasions. Intermarriages with other *gentes* became common. In this way the old independent villages became transformed into a tribal organization. When the villages became permanent, the defenses had to be of a powerful and permanent character.

Slaves had no economic importance in the old society; in the new one the reverse was true. This gave rise to more frequent raids for slaves and new methods of ransom. The old organization had made individual wealth impossible. Now subjects were stratified according to economic differences and a king was instituted. The old lineages retained only a ceremonial significance. Above all, the new organization placed new stresses on the adaptive powers of the individual. New interests, new goals and new conflicts were the consequences of the new society.

The king had arbitrary power over the life and property of everyone. There were taboos about his person and all other trappings of enhanced prestige and awe. On the other hand, he worked like a commoner in the fields. Land belonged to the king but was loaned on a revokable charter. A central power became necessary to control irrigation. In short, it became a feudal social order.

There were some interesting changes in mores and beliefs. Fear of sorcery was greatly augmented. The old religion of Tanala was lackadaisical. The new one conferred on the deity the ability to order everything in the life of everyone in advance. (This innovation is in accordance with the altered status of the father and king who formerly *did* arrange everything.) Sorcery became the cause of illness—indicating the operation of much envy and mutual hostility. Evil spirits abounded.

Spirit possession was much more common than in old Tanala. Malevolent sorcerers (*mpamosavy*) were quite frequent in the new society but uncommon in the old. Everyone was suspected of being a sorcerer. There was a great increase in general superstition and belief in charms: e.g., being too prosperous can be a cause of death. There was also a great increase in crime and in homosexuality.

These alterations in social patterning, for people whose adaptive equipment was geared to a different order, resulted in manifest signs of individual strain. Without some knowledge of psychodynamics it is impossible to account for these alterations of adaptive patterns and their manifestations, which occur with regularity wherever these types of social stresses are created.

The general level of individual anxiety was greatly augmented. The manifestations were great increases in superstition, largely protection against evil influences attributed to anonymous sources like sorcerers, evil spirits, etc. Who are these evil spirits? The people around them. This great increase of hatred, envy, and aggression, under some control, is a projective phenomenon. An individual's envy is perceived as an evil wish by someone else against him.

This situation was created by the fact that the personality, as developed in Tanala, was frustrated in the expectation of help from the entire community, which had been communally organized as far as subsistence was concerned. In some instances the aggressive tendencies broke out openly in increase in crime. The increase in *tromba,* the hysterical illness indigenous to the community, are the same hostile impulses under repressive control. Covert forms of aggression were also increased in the fear of and the practice of black magic (anonymous aggression). These people were not aggressive, but were trained in submissiveness and obedience. Suddenly they were called upon to become assertive and competitive, and only those whose constitutions were more aggressive could make the others submit. Fear was created when the individual was shorn of the communal protection he previously enjoyed and was completely on his own.

The alternatives are clearly drawn. Why was the aggression covert for the most part? One reason is that a majority of the people had not developed this capacity; those few who did have it assumed positions of leadership. A second reason is that *overt* aggression would lead to mutual extermination and the society would cease to exist.

We have noted the flight from masculinity in old Tanala—the transvestitism and homosexuality. What about homosexuality and its great increase in the new order? Homosexuality is not merely a sexual disorder. It is a serious miscarriage of adaptive devices, and there is no single theory that adequately accounts for its existence. Since the technique of ingratiation with the superior male paid off, homosexuality could easily represent an extension of this passivity. It could also represent the wish to incorporate the power of the father by oral or anal magical thinking. In any case homosexuality in this context must be regarded as a symptom of social *anomie*. This practice does not affect birth rate, especially in a society that tolerates polygamy. But when a large portion of males seek sexual satisfaction from other males and not women, it affects the relation between the sexes. It encourages polygamy, which has always been a corruption of the monogamous pattern by economic power or physical strength.

What we have discussed here is therefore a kind of *anomie* created by identifiable forces, and mediated through their impact on the human personality. The cross-cultural study of personality variations is therefore not an idle pastime, but the study of an important variable in the creation of social homeostasis or *anomie*. Increase in crime, hysterical and psychotic breakdowns, superstition, and homosexuality constitute therefore the quartet of manifestations of social breakdown.

We can now turn our attention to another situation taking place in our own country, and which ought to be called revolutionary, although violence is not now its conspicuous feature. I mean the Negro revolution, which is not restricted to the U.S.A. It is world wide, involving all underprivileged groups or national entities who cannot emulate the standards of life in the West. The collapse of colonialism is due to the unwillingness of colonial peoples to accept their inferior status any longer, whether because of skin color or lack of technological achievement.

But let us confine ourselves to the American Negro. For over three centuries the Negro accommodated himself to the conditions of slavery. The indigenes of North and South America could not do this. However, the Negro never accepted his status without some protest, ineffectual as it was. He could not take refuge in his own culture (as did the Jews) but had to adopt that of America without participation in it. The Civil War changed the legal status of the Negro but retained his position (in the South) as a source of cheap labor. His urbanization educated his sensibilities to events in the society as a whole, and stimulated him to want what the white man already had.

The cue for Negro assertiveness was, in all likelihood, the creation of the United Nations. There, many colored national entities were recognized and held political power in the world. In this body the U.S.A. was caught in a dilemma, from which the opportunity to escape came with the Supreme Court decision of 1954. American Negroes at last could follow the example set by may colonial peoples. They renounced their position of social inferiority and demanded immediate and full participation in our society as defined by the Constitution.

For an understanding of what motivates the Negro, it might be of some value to study the impact that the state of affairs before 1954 had on his personality. Freedom means unqualified access to opportunities that *exist* in a given society. In that sense the Negro had only limited freedom. The effect of this on personality formation is very tantalizing. Appetites are whetted, desires and needs stimulated, but opportunity to satisfy these legitimate cravings is lacking. The effect is collapse of *self-esteem*, or, more explicitly, self-hatred. The defeat is all the more complete because skin color is a very conspicuous element of identity. Self-hatred leads to hatred of others who share the same derogatory attributes—in this case, other Negroes. This destroys the inner cohesion of the group and prevents mutual co-operation. It also leads to the idealization of the white, whom they wish to emulate. Middle-class Negroes are more white in their mores than the whites themselves.

The amount of latent hatred in every Negro is enormous and has been kept under control for a long time. The Negro revolution was planned to prevent this aggression from becoming overt. For the most part, the Negro is trained to control his aggressive impulse, but recently it has been difficult for him to do so—sometimes impossible. The Uncle Toms are those in whom the aggression is successfully repressed and replaced by self-effacement, which can end only in the disappearance of all self-assertive trends.

The Negro revolution has partially discredited this control of self-assertion. Self-hatred and idealization of the whites can easily change to overt aggression. This is potentially a danger to our society.

I did not introduce the Negro problem to discuss the Negro issue, but merely to demonstrate the specific identifiable factors in the Negro adaptation to American culture that must be dealt with in order to restore the internal equilibrium of each Negro. Police force or common rejection of Negroes by whites can be effective only if the numbers are small. Twenty-two million is no longer a number that can be dealt with by police methods or intimidation. This creates a revolutionary situation.

You might ask at this point, what is so wrong about a segment of our population being in a perpetual state of rage? Rage is a general indicator that a need or a number of needs are not being satisfied. In the well-integrated personality, this can be tolerated so that it does not infest the entire personality. The special problem in the lower-class Negro is that the presence of this much tension in the personality during the period of growth impairs the effective development of the entire personality. The affectivity potential of the individual is particularly injured. This includes the ability to be dependent, to trust, to idealize; to become socially educable; to have the capacity for conscience and the capacity to love and be socially co-operative. This is what is wrong with a society that harbors a lot of angry people. Social co-operation in every aspect, private and public, becomes impaired.

Man is an integrative animal—that is, his adaptive tools are engrafted on an inherited potential by experience and learning on several strata of awareness. Social homeostats are among the things that are integrated in man. Society, not being an organism, has no automatic homeostats. They have to be built into the growing child. If these are not formed, the individual cannot be entreated, cajoled, preached at, or otherwise exhorted to *assume* characterological properties that failed to be built into him. He can only be intimidated and threatened. In that case you must make every member of the community a part of the police force (Orwell's *1984*). But such a society spends too much of its available energy just holding itself together. This blunts both the intelligence and enterprise of its constituents.

Having studied a large variety of social patterns and examined the end product, the human-personality-in-culture, I believe that not all forms of social patterning work out with equal degrees of effectiveness both for the individual or for the society. But so far as I know we are today the only society that ever existed that has sufficient knowledge self-correction. The inertia-obstructing self-correction comes largely from vested interests for whom, as far as they can see, the society is operating effectively. But even these interests are educable.

The trouble with my experience, however, is that it has been limited to simpler societies than our own, or to segments of our own society. There is too little application of psychodynamics to the data supplied by the social sciences to make it a valuable instrument of prediction. It is, notwithstanding its limited achievements to date, too valuable an instrument for the social sciences to ignore, in our time of urgency. It can pinpoint for us why a society like Alor is an almost complete failure.[2] Or it can tell us about where to direct our efforts to integrate the Negro.

The critical problem about the Negro revolution is to contain the potential collective rage that has been unleashed. This is recognized by some leaders of the revolution such as Martin Luther King. Monetary compensation could keep the lower-class Negro at peace, provided desegregation were a part of the total program.

Desegregation aims at eliminating discrimination and opens the possibility of full participation in the political and economic life of the nation. Another goal of the Negro revolution, the goal of integration, will not

[2] See Chapters V–IX in Abram Kardiner *et al.*, *The Psychological Frontiers of Society* (New York: Columbia University Press, 1945), which were based partially on the more lengthy account by Cora Du Bois, *The People of Alor* (Cambridge: Harvard University Press, 1960; and, New York: Harper and Row [Torchbooks], 1961; originally published by University of Minnesota Press).

be accomplished easily.[3] This goal is promoted chiefly by the upper classes of Negro society. "Integration defined as the elimination of differences demands of both Negroes and whites an impossible surrender of identity. The deletion of all memory of antecedents, the severance of all ties to the past, and the liquidation of all particularistic associations is not only unfeasible but undesirable."[4] Dr. Handlin believes that some of the advocates of integration are either nihilistic or would not flinch from totalitarian methods and consequences that would be involved in achieving this version of integration.

As evidence in favor of Dr. Handlin's position we can refer to the fact that some Negro spokesmen are now rejecting Martin Luther King's nonviolence policy for one of active aggression—to the end, presumably, of "self-defense."

From the point of view of psychodynamics, aggression can be impounded under certain conditions. It does not disappear but may be redirected against the Negro by himself. It may take the form of self-hatred, ending ultimately in total resignation. Once the aggression is detached from this socially safe mooring, it can then be—as is now recommended by some Negroes—directed against white society. They claim it is self-defensive in intent; but it can be transferred to another, more vindictive objective.

A situation like this may be termed revolutionary because the impounded aggression may be triggered. Outwardly directed aggression cannot, however, solve the problem of identity. I once had a patient who had

[3] See Oscar Handlin, "Goals of Integration," *Daedalus*, Winter 1966; reprinted in *Harvard Alumni Bulletin*, April 2, 1966, pp. 504–7.
[4] Handlin, *loc. cit.*

a serious identity disturbance. Its origins were complex but the disturbance was based on the issue of his Jewishness. His problem became to cease being a Jew. This seemed quite easy. He would have himself baptized in one of the Protestant denominations. He chose this group because they were collectively the most powerful social group. After his conversion, he felt Jewish. He tried a second and then a third denomination. He still felt Jewish. Finally, he abandoned the attempt to alter his identity.

By the same token the Negro cannot fight an identity problem with externalized aggression against whites: it involves a denial. By virtue of his past, the Negro has special problems which can better be solved by identification with his group. This may lead to more co-operation among Negroes. Whites will help him because they share his problems. Negro delinquency in a total community affects the total community.

Whether we can avoid some of the dangers lurking in the Negro revolution will become apparent with time. We now know that the locus of the trouble is the culture and personality development in the lower-class Negro family, as demonstrated by biographical studies.[5] It will take a long time to alter this situation. If the Negro resorts to violence, he will not escape the problem, but may well delay its solution.

[5] See A. Kardiner and L. Ovesey, *Mark of Oppression: Explorations in the Personality of the American Negro* (Cleveland: World Publishing Co. [Meridian paperback], 1961; originally published 1951).

EPILOGUE

SAMUEL Z. KLAUSNER

PROSPECTS FOR THE STUDY
OF TOTAL SOCIETIES

Research planning follows an expanding helix, describing everwidening curves about the axis of origin. The conference prospectus vaguely defined some problems in the study of total societies. There are problems generic to any such study: to what extent may a nation-state be considered a closed system for purposes of study and may relationships uncovered in one society be generalized to another; when would we use total societal measures (macrovariables) and when measures of social segments (microvariables); how may insights from various disciplinary perspectives be integrated; can images which people hold of their future state aid in understanding their present condition; which types of social action result from mechanical, deterministic processes and which depend upon values and voluntary choices; what are the respective advantages of equilibrium, dialectical, or accumulative change models for conceptualizing a total society; would a focus on institutions or a focus on social processes be a better way to initiate research on total societies? The papers have suggested methods for developing theory and of handling the data about total societies, and presented alternative substantive theories of social change and initial research strategies. Knowing these alternatives opens the way for a new helical cycle of research planning, the actual design for a study of a concrete total society. The work reported here has been a preparatory step toward such an actual design.

The contributors agree that, though one could never study everything about a society, it is possible (given our level of scientific development) to describe the present state and to predict future states of a total society. To execute such a study, the contributors agree that (1) a model of a total society might be constructed for heuristic purposes, (2) the model should focus upon processes of social change, and (3) the model should consider the dependence of events in a society upon external events as well as the relations among elements within a society. No contributor held that his approach invalidates another. Each approach offers its peculiar perspective on problems of research strategy. The methodological contributions will be summarized first, to be followed by summaries of the more substantive contributions.

The first methodological paper is concerned with analytical propositions or theoretical abstractions, while the remaining two papers in that section are concerned with empirical generalizations, involving more concretely observable variables, about a total society. Klausner asks how one may articulate disparate disciplinary perspectives in the study of total societies. Concepts derive their meaning, in part, from the theoretical networks in which they are embedded. Interdisciplinary propositions, those which link concepts on different levels, require specification of mechanisms by which, for example, a psychological conceptualization of an act is transformed or made relevant to a sociologically conceived act, or by which an economic act becomes relevant to a religious one. Most often, this requires specification of an institutional context, such as that of the family mediating religion and the economy.

It is then necessary to specify interaction in that context relevant to both of the disciplinary perspectives. The mediating mechanism may also be a symbol system which links, for example, the psychological and the social by reference to some shared meanings. Where this link is not specified, the manner in which, say, a psychological event influences a sociological event remains indeterminate.

Instead of analyzing an already functioning total society, Coleman proposed constructing an artificial model of a simplified social system. The construction is made manifest as a "game" involving actors and activities. Understanding is achieved by manipulating this simulated system and observing the outcomes. Specifically, his model is of the functioning of a political system in the context of a given economic system. This institutional juncture could be a point of entry into the total societal analysis. A system of production is established. For example, workers' labor is a first input; then a process such as mining leads to an output of raw materials. Rules are described for a mine owner offering these raw materials for sale to a manufacturer. Norms of the simulated social system evolve through this interaction. A symbolic description of the processes which emerge in this game constitutes a theory of a total society. Thus, the game is a way station between vague ideas and formal theory.

The game described presumes that processes of exchange, motivated according to rational considerations of self-interest, are at the heart of social change. To this extent, the initial design of the game, the "vague ideas," limit the types of theoretical outcome. However, the game is a heuristic device and another experimenter may begin with an alternate set of "vague ideas."

The computer has also been a heuristic device to suggest theory. For Pool, however, the computer is treated as a processing system to develop implications of a theory which a researcher already possesses. It is a thinking or calculating machine. Prerequisites for its exploitation in this manner are rigor in stating propositions, clear specification of what is related to what and with what probability, and a clear notion about how propositions are to be woven together. The rigor imposed upon the propositions tested and the computer's capacity for examination of vast amounts of information recommend it as an aid in the study of a total society. The implications appear as predictions to be checked with actuality.

The next three papers suggest alternative substantive models of societal change with which a researcher might approach the study of a total society. These and the papers on initial research strategy will be interpreted in terms of the basic image or metaphor informing each of them, the concepts of social change proposed, the types of observable indicators associated with these concepts, and points of entry suggested as initial research strategy.

Tiryakian grasps processes of change in the total society as a religious phenomenon. One part of his image is drawn from the religious experience of the individual and another from the religious institutional culture of a society. A conceptual dualism in which a physical-type secular world is counterposed to the spiritual runs through his presentation. Conceived through a physical metaphor, social change is a process of quantitative elaboration through structural differentiation. This is a mundane, continuous, cumulative process which proceeds until the system's limits of strain tolerance are reached. A threshold is passed, triggering the more exotic societal change. Societal change is essentially a religious transformation, an experience of death and rebirth. The society passes through something like the conversion experience of an individual, a qualitative change. A discontinuity occurs in the normative pattern of the society involving a restructuring of the society's organizations. The most fundamental aspect of societal change is a shift in the criteria of legitimation. The status quo is desacralized and new grounds of meaning are generated. The nonroutinized character of the organizational structure releases charismatic forces, through which institutions are renovated and cohesion re-established. Cataclysmic revolutionary change is accompanied by a societal catharsis, a drastic purification of the social structure. The nonroutinized character of the collective sentiments is a source of intense feeling. Violence may erupt if this feeling engages the sociopolitical sphere. If it engages the socioeconomic sphere, the transition may be more pacific.

Tiryakian suggests three initial indicators of incipient societal macrodynamics: these are changes in (1) rates of urbanization, (2) sexual attitudes, and (3) the rate of outbreak of noninstitutional religious phenomena. Rate of urbanization, an ecological indicator which may be assessed from census reports, has implications for rates of interaction which, in turn, affect social change. Further, the city is a seedbed for ideologies undermining routinized structures. Change in sexual attitudes, which may be assessed through analyses of written or interview materials, reveals readiness for delayed gratification, which, in turn, reflects commitment to the legitimacy of existing institutions which demand the delay. Change in the rate of outbreak of noninstitutional religious phenomena reflects the extent of tentative efforts at resolving strain in the religious institutional sphere which, in turn, parallels similar efforts in other institutional spheres.

Boulding's contribution is informed by a dialectical image of decay and restoration of the system. Society, in some respects, moves through repeated cyclical patterns. Economic consumption and production is an instance of this process. Social symbolic systems spread through symbolic epidemics and rise and fall in popularity. The restorative phase is marked by a change in the symbols held in society, a process Boulding calls macrolearning. The biological analogy stresses functional relations within the system. The macrolearning model attends more to the history of the system. The past bequeaths deposits of information to the present. These accumulate and, guided by a constant drive to parsimony based on relevancy, are sorted out. The accumulating information may pass a threshold beyond which the society is transfigured, that is, undergoes a qualitative change.

The study of decay and restoration of information over time serves as a lead-in to analysis of system dynamics. The researcher would study the people who mediate this communication, their lines of communication, and the changing population densities which affect the structure of communication. Boulding's information system is conceptualized in cybernetic terms. Structural changes reflect the balance of input-output relations. His indicators would be reports on where people are, what they are doing, and the types of symbols abroad in the society. He might consult population census material; maps showing the spatial distribution of the population; time budgets of individual activities and analyses of printed, aural, and pictorial mass media content during particular segments of time.

Rapoport offers both a formal model for studying any system and a substantive model for a social system. The formal model represents the state of any system by treating its data as points in space. The distribution of points in space may be analyzed through a spatial mathematical model. The economy, for example, may be represented by a "flow matrix."

His substantive model of a social system is an organismic one, based on a biological analogy. Social entities with discernible boundaries consist of functionally related parts. The researcher is encouraged to trace secular evolutionary change in society, watching for its mutations and being prepared to find vestigial institutions as one finds vestigial organs in biology. Evolutionary development of man is guided by psychological and social rather than simply biological factors. In fact, man uses intelligence to interfere with the operation of processes of biological natural selection in his own case. Types survive which are not biologically viable. Psychological and social or symbolic evolution differs from the biological. Cultural evolution proceeds more rapidly than biological and, therefore, cultural processes do not have time to eliminate dysfunctional elements. Consequently, no adaptive equilibrium can be achieved. New cultural features are not always adaptive for the whole society. They may even carry the seeds of a society's destruction. Rapoport calls for a higher level evolutionary theory subsuming both symbolic and biological evolution as instances.

In symbolic evolution, the specific units which change are intellectual. The "cognitive set" of a society, one of his core concepts, becomes a suggested point of entry for societal analysis. Cognitive set involves cultural belief systems. Culture cumulates through a process of "time-binding," to use Korzybski's term. When the cognitive set of a society becomes detached from reality, a kind of societal psychosis appears. Change in the cognitive set requires control of the "cultural gene pool," that is, of the knowledge by which the society operates.

To conceptualize the direction of change in the state of the total system, Rapoport speaks of the "trajectory of the system," a mathematical-physical, rather than an evolutionary, image. The trajectory depends upon cultural development. Thus, the study of cultural evolution is the significant lead-in to the study of total societal change. Initially, one would consider economic, military, religious or other institutional arrangements. Institutional arrangements condition social relations, and so the study of institutions leads to the study of social interaction and of social structure. Patterns of interaction, in turn, produce new institutional arrangements. This interplay between cultural institutions and social relations affects the trajectory of the system in ways which may or may not be functional for that system's survival.

Rapoport is not explicit about indicators for the study of total societies. Assumedly, following his suggestion to study institutional arrangements, he might collect verbal and written indicators of cultural norms and trace changes in their occurrence. Data generated by such a cultural analysis is amenable to matrix treatment. Computer simulation methods would allow simultaneous examination of variables from the several institutional spheres.

The evolutionary model presupposes progress and improvement with respect to the largest whole. One ignores the fate of the units which lose the struggle of natural selection. Rapoport introduces the possibility of total societal failure. Some element, though adaptive in a limited way, may bear the seed of the society's ultimate destruction. The nation-state, he feels, is one such dangerous development.

Etzioni's model of a total society is constructed by analogy to an electrical field of force. Nation-states are like conductors in various positions in this field. The movements of some induce current—that is, control—in others. The structure of power is central for understanding links among sectors of each society, and between them and sectors of other societies. Consequently, the problem of control is a suitable point of entry for the study of a total society. An institutional analysis follows specification of political, military, or economic sources of control. By studying the élites, who exert control, a picture of the social structure emerges. Analysis of the structure of dominance, the "muscles" of the society, reveals conditions for pursuing common goals, the commitment of a population, and has implications for union or disunion among societies. Etzioni suggests indicators of macrovariables, those characterizing the entire system, e.g., the trade balance in several countries, the number of élites in a political union and, for evidences of union, the criteria for allocating parliamentary seats.

Levy's image of a total society is designed to reduce the many to the few; he dimensionalizes and classifies as a first step. Holistic analysis requires development of generalized sets of theories in terms of a small number of variables. A recurrent image reflects a tension between the immanent attainable and the idealized unattainable. Analytic structural variables, ideal-typical in nature, are contrasted with actual concrete organizational conditions. Actual norms, what people do, are distinguished from ideal norms, society's expectations of what people should do.

A study of the family provides a lead-in to total societal analysis. The family is strategic because of its links with other social institutions. Family socialization of the child is the cradle of socialization for other institutions. Beginning with the learning process, like Rapoport and Boulding, Levy would be initially concerned with symbol systems.

While concerned with symbolic interaction, Levy would recognize the consequences of mechanical factors. These include, for example, the imperatives of number in a population. The ratio of male to female births has predictable societal consequences. His research indicators are both macrosociological and microsociological. The presence or absence of medical technology is a global characteristic of a collective that directly reflects the total society. A measure of relations among people in a household—a structural characteristic of a small unit—may be aggregated to become a description of a total society.

Limiting conditions should be recognized. Ideal norms never can coincide with actual norms. If everybody always knew what to do, there would be cognitive overload and more information would have to be stored by each individual than he would be capable of. From a societal point of view, the system would become too brittle and lose the flexibility inherent in the possibility of deviating from the ideal norm. Levy is less concerned here with new observations than with cautioning scientists to interpret intelligently the observations they have already made.

Kardiner's working image is of pressure on an elastic body, that of social institutions on the character of man. Man's changing behavior manifests his attempts to cope with these pressures. Kardiner would initiate a study of a total society with an investigation of the man-institution relation. Coping involves maintaining an internal equilibrium by striving for an equilibrium between himself and his institutional environment. A change in family, in religion, in the economy, or in the organization of power, affects man's propensity to relate to others passively or actively, or with hostility or friendliness.

Institutions seek a homeostatic balance among themselves. Change in the economy leads to change in patterns of human settlement, in organization for defense, and in the structure of relations among members of the population. Social homeostats, according to Kardiner, depend on individual ones. The individual's homeostats may be damaged or inadequate when man is exposed to a severe shift in institutional requirements. Then, he may fail to cope with institutional pressure. He suffers anxiety which he tries to alleviate by pressing for institutional change or by withdrawing into magical activities. The individual shorn of communal protection experiences fear, frustration, and rage. His self-esteem and ability to give and receive affection are damaged. Kardiner would initiate research on a total society with a study of institutional—especially occupational—conditions and individual personalities. Kardiner's indicators include observations on how individuals make their living and the impact of their work situation on their behavior in other institutional spheres. Psychological aspects of behavior, such as aggressiveness and religious beliefs, would be examined in this institutional context.

If society constitutes a system, to study anything about it is, in principle, to take cognizance of a total society. An understanding of microsocial elements involves studying the influence upon them of molar societal characteristics. A study of a total society as such directly emphasizes these molar characteristics, which

involve gross movements of the social body. Molar
characteristics of a nation-state are, for example, its
going to war, its particular political complexion, its
type of economic organization or the character of its
religion. Independent variables affecting these molar
characteristics may themselves be molar characteristics
of the same or of another society. Independent variables may also be relatively molecular changes within
that society, such as changing attitudes of members of
its élite, or changing types of raw materials available.

Many methodological problems of molar societal
analysis are also encountered in molecular analysis. A
concrete study of a small group might also require, for
example, statements that bridge disciplines. A total societal study is distinguished not only by the presence
of molar variables but also by the fact that intrasystemic factors alone explain more than they would in
the case of a subsystem. The total system boundary is
less permeable—though not impermeable, as Etzioni
has shown—than the subsystem boundary.

Most of the discussion in this volume has concerned
problems that arise in any study of any total society.
The decision to use macroanalysis rather than micro-
analysis can be resolved only in terms of the purposes
of any given concrete study. Similarly, essential decisions about data gathering cannot be made "in general." It is probably inefficient to attempt to gather an
exhaustive set of societal indicators useful for any contingent study. Aside from the indeterminateness of the
term "exhaustive," too many items crucial for one purpose are irrelevant for another. One must pick processes of interest in terms of a particular goal or a particular theory, and gather indicators for them.

Though no single study or set of indicators can suit
all purposes, it is possible to monitor a total society for
signs of incipient distress. Just as a physician may take

strategic measures as indicators of the over-all "health" of a biological system, one may obtain strategic measures of the "health" of a society. Of course, to define physical "health" is relatively simple in view of our social consensus on the desirability of survival of the organism and of maintaining particular levels of functioning. To assess the "health" of a society entangles one in social philosophy. By "health," one does not usually intend an objective state but rather the efficiency of societal functioning with respect to value goals. A society may function in many ways. It may be a "healthy" capitalist or socialist society, a "healthy" autocracy or democracy. This symposium does not seriously engage these value issues. Particular foci of interest emerge, however, from resolutions of these value issues which direct the researcher in ways of monitoring the "health" of society. It may be of interest to study religious development, economic development, or the potential for revolutionary change of the political structure. Having selected one, or two, or some small number of macrovariables, the study would proceed by investigating its ramifications—and only its proximate ramifications—on several disciplinary levels and across several institutional spheres. If, for example, the degree of industrialization is the focal macrovariable, it might be efficient to proceed to an assessment of economic imagery and problems of its legitimation in terms of Boulding's macrolearning model; to look at the interdependence of the economy and systems of political control using Etzioni's concepts of political unification; to study psychodynamic changes in the individual in the wake of changes in occupational patterns, using Kardiner's model of institutional-individual relations; and draw upon Levy's study of family socialization to assess the socially structured motivational resources for industrialization. Feedback and recycling of influences would be considered. An economic change may produce a change in the individual personalities of members of the society. These changed personalities might then present new problems on the economic level. If, for example, hostile motivation were to accompany an industrial innovation, as it did in Kardiner's example, then the establishment of co-operative work relations within a factory system would become more difficult. If, because of changes in economic relations, there were to be changes in bases of legitimacy, as Tiryakian suggests, then the political theorist would have to deal with a changing power structure. These are some paths from the suggested points of entry into the social network.

Earlier attempts to describe a total society tended to rest upon single factors: the relation of individuals to the means of production; religious conversion; or climatic shifts. The present generation of scientists is committed to multifactor analysis and prepared to deal not only with structure at a point in time, but with structure over time, with process. It is prepared to take the system view of Rapoport and recognize the changing values of parameters and even change the parameters themselves in the course of the process. Max Weber's "historical individual" was a precursor of this type of thinking since it emphasized the achievement of a pattern of factors. More recently, Neil Smelser's "value added" model has taken the notion of a pattern of variables at several levels and added a time sequence dimension. A particular type of collective behavior occurs when a succession of prior events has been realized. With this stochastic type of data modeling and rigorous propositions, one is ready, as Pool proposes, to test complex models of a total society with methods of computer simulation.

INDEX